THE HEART SUTRA AND BEYOND

ALSO BY KWAN-YUK CLAIRE SIT

The Lord's Prayer
An Eastern Perspective

Lao Tzu and Anthroposophy
*A Translation of the Tao Te Ching with Commentary
and a Lao Tzu Document "The Great One Excretes Water"*

The Heart Sutra *and* Beyond

Kwan-yuk Claire Sit

薛羅君鈺

Lindisfarne Books | 2014

2014
Lindisfarne Books
An imprint of SteinerBooks, Inc.
610 Main Street, Great Barrington, MA 01230
www.steinerbooks.org

Copyright © 2014 Kwan-yuk Claire Sit

All rights reserved. No part of this book may be reproduced, stored in a retrieval system, or transmitted in any form or by any means, electronic, mechanical, photocopying, recording, or otherwise, without the written permission of Lindisfarne Books.
Author photo copyright © by Emil Sit, 2008
Book and cover design by William Jens Jensen

LIBRARY OF CONGRESS CONTROL NUMBER 2014946427

ISBN 978-1-58420-173-1 (Paperback)
ISBN 978-1-58420-174-8 (eBook)

Contents

The Heart Sutra
   In Chinese   1
   In English   3

Introduction   5

Chapter 1
   Bodhisattva   13
   Bodhisattva Avalokitesvara   14
   Prajnaparamita   19
   Light Is Empty   21

Chapter 2
   Sariputra   25
   Form and Emptiness   28
   Essence and Nothingness   29
   Sierpinski Triangle   30
   Buddha's Silence on Creation   32
   Higher Beings Create Forms in Light   34

Chapter 3
   Dharma Negations   37
   Early Buddhism   40
   Zen Buddhism   44
   Calligraphy of The Heart Sutra   47
   The Koan of Raising a Finger   49

Chapter 4
   The Bodhisattva Path   51
   Buddhas in the Three Times   57
   Buddhism and Anthroposophy   60

Chapter 5
   Mantras   67
   The Prajnaparamita Mantra   71
   Great Blessings   73

Appendix: A Brief Introduction to Anthroposophy   75
Selected Bibliography   85
Index   89

I see light
Light delights me
Light and I are one
Light lives in me

The Heart Sutra

In Chinese

Translated from Sanskrit by Master Xuánzàng 玄奘法師 (602–664)

觀自在菩薩, 行深般若波羅蜜多時, 照見五蘊皆空, 度一切苦厄。

舍利子, 色不異空, 空不異色, 色即是空, 空即是色, 受想行識, 亦復如是。

舍利子, 是諸法空相, 不生不滅, 不垢不淨, 不增不減。是故空中無色, 無受想行識, 無眼耳鼻舌身意, 無色聲香味觸法, 無眼界, 乃至無意識界。無無明, 亦無無明盡, 乃至無老死, 亦無老死盡。無苦集滅道, 無智亦無得。

以無所得故, 菩提薩埵, 依般若波羅蜜多故, 心無罣礙, 無罣礙故, 無有恐怖, 遠離顛倒夢想, 究竟涅槃。三世諸佛, 依般若波羅蜜多故, 得阿耨多羅三藐三菩提。

故知般若波羅蜜多, 是大神咒, 是大明咒, 是無上咒, 是無等等咒, 能除一切苦, 真實不虛, 故說般若波羅蜜多咒, 即說咒曰,

揭諦, 揭諦, 波羅揭諦, 波羅僧揭諦, 菩提薩婆訶。

In English

Translated from Xuánzàng's Chinese text

Bodhisattva Avalokitesvara, while absorbed in the profundity of the perfection of wisdom, illuminated the five aggregates and beheld them all empty. He transcended all pain and suffering.

Listen, Sariputra, form is no different from emptiness, and emptiness is no different from form. Whatever is form is emptiness and whatever is emptiness is form. The same holds for feeling, thinking, willing, and discerning.

Here, Sariputra, all dharmas are a semblance of emptiness that is neither produced nor destroyed, neither defiled nor cleansed, and neither increased nor decreased. Therefore, in emptiness there is neither form, nor feeling, nor thinking, nor willing, nor discerning; neither eye, ear, nose, tongue, body, nor mind; neither form, sound, smell, taste, tactility, nor mental objects; neither a field of vision nor even a field of cognition. There is neither ignorance nor an end to ignorance, neither aging and death nor an end to aging and death. There is no suffering, no cause of suffering, no extinction of suffering, and no path to an end of suffering. There is no knowledge and no attainment.

Without aiming for attainment, and only relying on the perfection of wisdom, bodhisattvas find no obstacles in the mind. With no obstacles, they have no fear. They depart afar from inverted delusions, and eventually enter nirvana. Relying on the perfection of wisdom, all buddhas in the Three Times fully awaken to the unexcelled-complete-universal enlightenment.

Therefore one should know that the perfection of wisdom is the great spiritual mantra, the mantra of great understanding, the supreme mantra, and the mantra equal to the unequalled. It can allay all suffering and is the truth not falsehood. By the prajna-paramita has this mantra been extolled and it says:

Gate, gate, paragate, parasamgate, bodhi svaha!

Introduction

The *Prajnaparamita Sutras* (般若波羅蜜多經), or briefly *The Prajna Sutras* (般若經), form a collection of six hundred Buddhist sutras whose common theme is about the perfection of wisdom (*prajnaparamita* 般若波羅蜜多). *The Prajnaparamita Heart Sutra* (般若波羅蜜多心經), commonly known as *The Prajna Heart Sutra* or just *The Heart Sutra* (*Xīn Jīng* 心經), is a compendium that distills the essence of this great volume.

The Heart Sutra discusses the empty nature of a human being's core existence, concisely explains the teachings of Buddhism, and provides a mantra that can allay all suffering and enable enlightenment. *The Heart Sutra* is popular among practicing Buddhists and lay people alike. Many would recite it for comfort and guidance.

When I first came across *The Heart Sutra* decades ago, I was puzzled by one of its statements: "form is no different from emptiness, and emptiness is no different from form." Form and emptiness appear so diametrically opposite, how can they be no different from each other? Furthermore, the statement itself also seems to be a form of emptiness—empty of substantial meanings! At that time, I was only a beginning and casual reader of Buddhist scriptures. It was imprudent of me to draw a hasty opinion on this sacred text. Through the years, I have perused a broader array of Buddhist literature with the intent to deepen my understanding of this sutra and especially to resolve that puzzle.

Coincidently, I have a copy of the calligraphy rubbing of *The Heart Sutra* in Chinese by the famous calligrapher Ōuyáng Xún 歐陽

詢 (557–641).¹ I regularly practice calligraphy with this rubbing, timidly hoping that the exercise may improve my penmanship and award me with a greater insight into this sutra. It is disappointing that my years of effort have not produced any significant results as anticipated.

Buddhist teachings maintain that there is no creator. Instead, they introduce the theory of *dependent origination* (*yuán-qǐ* 緣起) to explain that things and events arise owing to their inter-depending causations. However, this theory is inadequate because it does not clarify why there are inter-depending causations to begin with. My inquisitive mind drove me to delve into other schools of knowledge for more satisfactory explanations. It was gratifying that I came across Anthroposophy that explores issues not addressed in Buddhism.

Then, while on a trip during the New Year break of 2012, I suffered a short yet severe spell of insomnia. For several days, I had only a few catnaps, felt extremely groggy, and could hardly function normally. I resorted to copying and reciting *The Heart Sutra* and pondering on it. Such intensive immersion with the text created unexpectedly a tipping point, motivating me to analyze this sutra with approaches, which are partly traditional and partly unconventional. Let me outline here five observations I used in these various approaches:

- First, *Guān-zì-zài* 觀自在, the translation for Avalokitesvara, literally signifies the main theme of this whole sutra (chapter 1).
- Second, *Shè-lì-zi* 舍利子, the translation for Sariputra, literally represents a practitioner's spiritual advancement, threading through different topics of this sutra (chapters 2 to 5).
- Third, *The Heart Sutra* teaches concisely Mahayana Buddhism (a later school of Buddhism) and touches on Hinayana Buddhism (the early Buddhist teachings) from a negative perspective (chapter 3).²

---

1   See chapter 3 for additional comments about this artwork.
2   Many Buddhists prefer the term *Theravada* ("teachings of the elders") today in place of *Hinayana,* which is considered pejorative by some.

- Fourth, Anthroposophy is indeed an intelligent body of knowledge, which clarifies the mystery between form and emptiness (chapters 1 and 2).
- Fifth, Anthroposophy also teaches that the religious streams of Buddhism and esoteric Christianity are subtly entwined. It shows the special relationship between Gautama Buddha with the boy Jesus, and the profound connection between Jesus Christ and the future Maitreya Buddha (chapter 4).

Anthroposophy is a comprehensive study of the spiritual world propagated by the Austrian spiritual teacher Rudolf Steiner (1861–1925), who taught extensively on how human beings and the cosmos are interrelated and how they evolve in parallel.[3] According to Steiner, cosmic knowledge used to be a human heritage. In antiquity, people had some mystically blurred form of clairvoyance to gaze into the spiritual world, and hence would know the influence of the cosmos. This clairvoyance, however, slowly declined when the human soul started its development. The soul consists of three elements: the sentient soul, the intellectual (or mind) soul, and the consciousness soul. Each element slowly develops one after another. (See the appendix for more information.) When human beings developed their sentient soul from around 3000 to 800 BCE, this blurred form of clairvoyance gradually diminished, and it was almost gone when they developed their intellectual soul around 800 BCE. Only a small number of initiates could still observe the spiritual world, but they did not openly disclose their visions. Gautama Buddha (c. 563–483 BCE), also known as Buddha Shakyamuni or simply the Buddha, was obviously one such initiate.

Nowadays, human beings have satisfactorily developed their mind soul to reason logically and they are ready to perceive the spiritual world with intellectually clear clairvoyance. Whereas in

---

3   See the appendix for a brief introduction of Anthroposophy.

the past all human beings were endowed with some clairvoyance, however, in modern times, human beings have to cultivate this ability by themselves. Anthroposophy reintroduces cosmic knowledge into human consciousness, thus paving a way for humankind to reconnect with the spiritual realm.

Steiner also taught that after the Mystery of Golgotha (the death and resurrection of Jesus Christ), the Christ spirit or the Cosmic Christ was planted in the human heart like a seed waiting to germinate and manifest. That which is referred to as the Cosmic Christ by Christians is intrinsically no different from that which is referred to as the Cosmic Buddha or buddha nature by Buddhists, or the *Tao* by Taoists. How *The Heart Sutra* teaches Buddhists to realize buddha nature may also be adopted to teach Christians to realize the Christ spirit, or Taoists to realize the *Tao*. Therefore, studying *The Heart Sutra* through the prism of Anthroposophy may benefit spiritual aspirants of different religious traditions.

The development of Buddhism is based on the teachings of Gautama Buddha. However, none of Buddha's sermons was recorded during his lifetime. After his passing, his disciples convened their first council and decided to compile Buddha's teachings in writings. Ananda (*Ānán* 阿難), Buddha's cousin and personal attendant, was renowned for his unfailing memory and he contributed significantly to this undertaking. These works establish the following scripture writing style: a beginning sentence: "Thus have I heard" (如是我聞), to indicate that what was recorded was exactly what the Buddha had expounded, then the descriptions of the location, the assembly, the individual who initiated the topic under discussion, the discourse on the topic, and a summary of the discussion, finally ending with a hymn.

The earlier scriptures were written in Pali (a vernacular language) and the later ones were written in Sanskrit (a learned language). Though Buddhism gradually had disappeared in India, Buddhism was and has been devotedly practiced in other eastern parts of Asia.

Introduction

Many Sanskrit Buddhist texts were lost, but fortunately, most of these works had been meticulously translated into Chinese when Buddhism was still at its height in the Indian subcontinent. Thus the Chinese translations are generally regarded as the canonical Buddhist documents.

The version of *The Heart Sutra*, which we use in this commentary, consists of only the discourse and is at a variant with the aforementioned general Buddhist writing format. In his book *Bō-rě Xīn Jīng Sī Xiǎng Shǐ* 般若心經思想史 (*Thought History of The Prajna Heart Sutra*; no English edition is known), Dong Chu Old Monk 東初老和尚 (1907–1977) observes that *The Heart Sutra*, which is not part of the great *Prajna Sutras*, reads similar to some passages there. He concludes that this short sutra is probably an extract from the great *Prajna Sutras*.[4] Nevertheless, there is a longer version of this sutra that follows the Buddhist writing format. That longer version is essentially similar to this short one except for the added beginning and ending narrations.[5]

In his book, Dong Chu Old Monk traces the translation history of this short version of *The Heart Sutra* to the Song Dynasty (960–1279) and is able to list at least eleven Chinese translations. Among these eleven translations the fourth and fifth were lost.[6] On the other hand, the two earliest translations are still widely perused and indeed the second translation has become the standard version. Let us briefly review the status of these two earliest versions and the background of their translators.

---

4   See *Bō-rě Xīn Jīng Sī Xiǎng Shǐ* 般若心經思想史, chapter 3, or its electronic version, pp. 288–293; at www.jingshu.org/article-9123-1.html.

5   See, for example, Sonam, *The Heart Sutra: An Oral Teaching by Geshe Sonam Rinchen*; see also, *The Heart of the Perfection of Wisdom Sutra*, www.angelfire.com/mt/thubtentenzin/page4.html.

6   See *Bō-rě Xīn Jīng Sī Xiǎng Shǐ*, chapter 5 or its electronic version, p. 296 at www.jingshu.org/article-9123-1.html.

The first translator of *The Heart Sutra*, Kumarajiva 鳩摩羅什 (334–413 or 350–409) was born in Kucha (*Qiū-cí* 龜茲), a little country on the Silk Road branch. He became a Buddhist monk at age seven, and later settled in China. He was versatile in both Sanskrit and Chinese and his overall Buddhist scripture translations are highly praised for their elegant prose style. Nevertheless, his rendition of *The Heart Sutra* is not as popular as the one by the second translator Xuánzàng 玄奘 (602–664).[7]

Xuánzàng became a Buddhist monk at age thirteen, went to India in his late twenties, and stayed there for about sixteen years to further his study of Buddhism. Returning to China in 645, he brought back more than six hundred Buddhist works and was only able personally to translate a portion of them. He translated *The Heart Sutra* in 649.[8] It is noteworthy that Xuánzàng advocated a "five no-translation rule" which described five types of Sanskrit terms that should not be translated but only transcribed,[9] and that he translated Laozi's *Tao Te Ching* into Sanskrit and sent it to India in year 647.[10]

The translated works of both Kumarajiva and Xuánzàng contributed significantly to the flowering of Mahayana Buddhism in China. It is ironic that nowadays none of Xuánzàng's other translations are as popular as his translation of *The Heart Sutra*, while several of Kumarajiva's translations other than *The Heart Sutra* are still frequently read.

---

7   You may read this first rendition, which some Buddhist scholars attributed to a student of Kumarajiva's, at www.baike.baidu.com/view/1144930.htm.

8   See, for instance, a chronological list of Xuánzàng's translated works by Dan Lusthaus, www.acmuller.net/yogacara/thinkers/xuanzang-works-uni.htm.

9   For the five types of Sanskrit terms, see *Transcription into Chinese Characters*, paragraph on "History" at www.en.wikipedia.org/wiki/Transcription_into_Chinese_characters.

10 See *Xuanzang*, paragraph on *His Return to China and Career as Translator (645–664);* www.iep.utm.edu/xuanzang/#H3.

Introduction

Indeed, Xuánzàng's translation of *The Heart Sutra* is concise, articulate, fluent, and easy to recite. It is fondly cherished and even has been made into a popular Cantonese song.[11] While preparing this commentary on Xuánzàng's translation, I have consulted a wide spectrum of Buddhist and Anthroposophy literature, which markedly broadens my horizons during my reading of *The Heart Sutra* and amply enriches my writing experience.[12]

A Special Note: The Chinese names and terms are romanized using the pinyin system. Yet, we keep the Wade-Giles forms that appear in bibliographical entries. As for Sanskrit terms we adopt the common English phonetic equivalents as in many recent popular Buddhist writings.

Acknowledgement

Thanks to the staff members of SteinerBooks for facilitating the publication of this book, especially to William Jens Jensen for the book and cover design, editing, and a summary of Steiner's twelve senses on page 42.

---

11 You may sample performances of this song on YouTube.com.

12 By the way, all quoted Buddhist scriptures in this book are based on the Chinese texts and their English versions are my interpretation, with the exception in chapter 1 of two passages from *The Surangama Sutra (Léng-yán Jīng* 楞嚴經*)*, which are taken from http://www.fodian.net/world/shurangama.html.

Chapter 1

觀自在菩薩，行深般若波羅蜜多時，照見五蘊皆空，度一切苦厄。

Bodhisattva Avalokitesvara, while absorbed in the profundity of the perfection of wisdom, illuminated the five aggregates and beheld them all empty. He transcended all pain and suffering.

Bodhisattva

The Sanskrit term *Bodhisattva* consists of two words: *bodhi* and *sattva*. While the word *sattva* may mean either any sentient being or all living beings, the word *bodhi* depending on the context, can mean knowledge, understanding; perfect wisdom; the illuminated or enlightened mind; to be aware, perceive. The term *bodhisattva* means a sentient being striving for the great enlightenment or perfect wisdom. According to Buddhist traditions, a bodhisattva (*pú-tí-sà-duǒ* 菩提薩埵 or *pú-sà* 菩薩 for short) is an enlightened compassionate being who benefits self to benefit others (*zì-lì-lì-tā* 自利利他).[1]

The term *bodhisattva* is closely related to another Sanskrit term, *buddha*, which means "a completely conscious and enlightened being."[2] Traditionally, an individual who is completely awakened and fully at one with *bodhi* (perfect wisdom) is called a *buddha*, and one who is still on the path toward complete awakening is called a bodhisattva. Henceforth, we broadly regard as equivalent terms

---

1 See Soothill and Hodous (eds.), *A Dictionary of Chinese Buddhist Terms with Sanskrit and English Equivalents and a Sanskrit-Pali Index*, p. 467b, p. 388b, and p. 389a.
2 Ibid., p. 225a.

such as *perfect wisdom, wisdom, reality, Universal Consciousness, Consciousness, Intelligence, the Absolute, God,* and *Tao.*

Buddhism teaches that in the transition from a bodhisattva to a buddha a process of fifty-two steps is required. When individuals become enlightened, they have a chance to enter *nirvana* (*niè-pán* 涅槃). The Sanskrit term *nirvana* may mean "extinguished," "liberated from existence," or "eternal bliss." In Buddhism, it means "liberation from the cycle of *samsara*" (*shēng-sǐ* 生死, birth and death). However, bodhisattvas dedicate themselves to become completely enlightened but vow not to enter nirvana until all beings are enlightened. For instance, Rinpoche Chögyam Trungpa made a vow to "remain a Bodhisattva without entering Nirvana so long as a single blade of grass remains unenlightened."[3]

According to Buddhist teachings, Gautama Buddha (c. 563–483 BCE) is considered the buddha in the present eon; many buddhas had existed before him, and many more will appear after him. During Gautama Buddha's lifetime, some highly enlightened disciples of the ancient buddhas were incarnated on Earth as his followers. Bodhisattva Avalokitesvara was one such highly enlightened being.[4]

Bodhisattva Avalokitesvara

Avalokitesvara means literally *the Lord of Observation* and is sometimes shortened to *Avalokita*. Kumarajiva 鳩摩羅什 (334–413 or 350–409) and Xuánzàng 玄奘 (602–664), two early translators of *The Herat Sutra* (see the introduction for a brief account of both), translated this name differently. Kumarajiva translated *Avalokitesvara* as *Guān-shì-yīn* 觀世音 and Xuánzàng translated it as *Guān-zì-zài* 觀自在. We discern that the translation *Guān-shì-yīn* interprets

---

3   Chögyam Trungpa, *Born in Tibet*, p. 56. We do not capitalize terms such as *bodhisattva, buddha, maya,* and *nirvana*, except when they are used as a proper noun or when they appear capitalized in the quoted text.

4   Buddhist teachings mention four great bodhisattvas: Avalokitesvara (*Guānyīn* 觀音), Manjusri (*Wénshū* 文殊), Samantabhadra (*Pǔxián* 普賢), and Kshitigarbha (Decáng 地藏).

Chapter 1

Avalokitesvara as an observer of sound, whereas the translation *Guān-zì-zài* interprets him as an observer of light.

Let us first inspect the meaning of the name *Guān-shì-yīn*. The word *guān* 觀 means to look, to observe; the word *shì* 世, the world; and the word *yīn* 音, sounds. Together, the name *Guān-shì-yīn* means an observer of the world's sounds.

This translated name *Guān-shì-yīn* is often shortened to *Guān-yīn*. It was said that the shortened form was in deference to the emperor Taizong of Tang Dynasty 唐太宗 (598–649), whose given name Li Shì-Mín 李世民 contained the word *shì* 世, a taboo to be avoided. This may just be a speculation because Chinese scriptures use both the full and shortened forms liberally. Probably, *Guān-shì-yīn* 觀世音 was shortened to *Guān-yīn* 觀音, just as *pú-tí-sà-duǒ* 菩提薩埵 was shortened to *pú-sà* 菩薩.

Gautama Buddha says that when people are in distress they can get help from Bodhisattva Avalokita by calling upon him and chanting his name.

> Suppose that there are immeasurable hundreds, thousands, ten thousands, hundred millions of living beings who are undergoing various sufferings and afflictions. If they have heard of this Bodhisattva Avalokita and single-mindedly call his name, then at once he will perceive the sound of their voices and they will all get rescued.
> (若有無量百千萬億眾生, 受諸苦惱, 聞是觀世音菩薩, 一心稱名, 觀世音菩薩, 即時觀其音聲, 皆得解脫。)[5]

Gautama Buddha additionally provides many details on how Bodhisattva Avalokita "takes on a variety of different forms, goes among the lands, and rescues living beings" (以種種形、遊諸國土, 度脫眾生).[6] By rescuing living beings, it is meant delivering them from

---

5   *The Lotus Sutra* (*Fǎhuá Jīng* 法華經), ch. 25.
6   Ibid.

their pressing trials, endowing them enlightenment, and freeing them from the cycle of samsara (birth and death).

Once in an assembly, Bodhisattva Avalokita reported to Gautama Buddha that eons ago a buddha by the name of Tathagata Observer of Sounds (*Guān-yīn Rú-lái* 觀音如來)[7] taught him "to meditate using a process of hearing and reflecting" (從聞思修):

> Initially, I entered into the flow of hearing and forgot the place of entry. Since both that place and the entry were quiet, the two attributes of motion and stillness cancelled each other out and did not arise. After that, gradually advancing, the hearing and what was heard both disappeared. Once the hearing was ended, there was nothing to rely on, and both awareness and its objects became empty. When the emptiness of awareness was ultimately perfected, emptiness and what was being emptied then also ceased to be. With arising and ceasing gone, tranquility was revealed.
> (初於聞中，入流亡所。所入既寂，動靜二相了然不生。如是漸增。聞所聞盡。盡聞不住。覺所覺空。空覺極圓。空所空滅。生滅既滅。寂滅現前。)[8]

In that assembly, Bodhisattva Avalokita further recounts how he diligently practiced another meditation technique that Tathagata Observer of Sounds taught and then he discloses:

> I obtained the perfect penetration of the sense organ and have discovered the wonder of the ear-entrance, after which my body and mind subtly and miraculously included all of the Dharma Realm.
> (由我所得圓通本根，發妙耳門。然後身心微妙含容，周遍法界。)[9]

---

[7] There are ten titles for a buddha, and *Tathagata* (*Rú-lái* 如來) is one of them; see chapter 4, page 56 for an interpretation of this title.

[8] *The Surangama Sutra* (*Léngyán Jīng* 楞嚴經), ch. 6. See www.fodian.net/world/shurangama.html for the English translation.

[9] Ibid.

Chapter 1

Thousand-hand Guān-yīn: *This wooden statue was created in Bac Ninh Province of Northern Vietnam around 1656 for the But Thap Pagoda (image reframed from a photo at wikipedia.org/wiki/Guanyin).*

Thus he attained an aptitude of compassion equal to that of all buddhas, possessed the power to rescue beings in any form and in any land, and knew all mantras.

Because of Avalokitesvara's miraculous achievements, he can hear all those who call him for help, and in his response to their call he may appear in a variety of different forms, female or male, human or non-human. However, people seem to prefer the appearance of Avalokitesvara as a mother goddess and in the so-called thousand-hand form. Perhaps people feel more akin to a mother and regard her inexhaustible ability to help as coming from someone with a thousand hands.[10]

The populace reveres Avalokitesvara as a beloved goddess of mercy. She has entwined with the livelihood of humankind through and through. It is reported that at times of imminent danger, the chanting of "Homage to Bodhisattva Avalokitesvara" (*Nā-mó Guān-shì-yīn pú-sà* 南無觀世音菩薩) is especially effective; rescue will occur right away. We infer that when people single-mindedly call upon her name in distress, they become "selfless" at that moment. Hence, they instantly merge into Universal Consciousness and realize a miraculous relief. As people are generally too self-centered to be selfless, they can hardly merge into Universal Consciousness. Now through the immense mercy of Bodhisattva Avalokitesvara, people in distress can gain immediate relief if they wholeheartedly invoke her name.

Esotericism teaches that practitioners can develop spiritual ear or spiritual eye to observe the sound or light attribute of Consciousness.[11] Bodhisattva Avalokita excels at observing with both spiritual organs. Obviously, the name *Guān-yīn* refers to her observation of sound with the spiritual ear. Indeed, she reports that she has discovered the wonder of the (spiritual) ear-entrance.

Here, the beginning passage of *The Heart Sutra* indicates that in deep meditation Avalokitesvara observes light (with the spiritual eye): "The bodhisattva Avalokitesvara, while absorbed in the profundity of the perfection of wisdom, illuminated the five aggregates and beheld them all empty" (觀自在菩薩, 行深般若波羅蜜多時, 照見五蘊皆空). We shall learn that at the end of *The Heart Sutra* Avalokitesvara teaches a mantra for meditation on

---

10 See the image of the thousand-hand Avalokitesvara on page 17; also watch a dance inspired by such an appearance at www.youtube.com/watch?v=9FdEKzOnoGc.

11 For information about the development of spiritual organs, see the following section "Light Is Empty"; see also chapter 3, footnote 6.

Chapter 1

sound. Nonetheless, the sutra mainly focuses on describing her inner vision of light and the consciousness without knowledge of an object during deep meditation.

Let us now analyze the significance of the name *Guān-zì-zài* 觀自在. The word *guān* 觀, as stated earlier, means to look, to observe. The word *zì* 自 means the self; and the word *zài* 在, existence. Hence, *Guān-zì-zài* 觀自在 means an observer of one's ground of existence. In Chinese, the term *zì-zài* 自在 conveys the idea of feeling comfortable and usually implies feeling unrestrained and free (*zì-yóu* 自由) as well. Hence the term *zì-zài* is a shortened expression for *zì-yóu-zì-zài* 自由自在 meaning feeling free and comfortable. Therefore, the name *Guān-zì-zài* connotes that Avalokitesvara is observing her ground of existence, feeling free and comfortable, thus transcending all pain and suffering.

Now, the foundation of one's existence is Consciousness. Symbolically, every entity exists in the sea of Consciousness. Sentient beings on Earth are like an ice patch that has been frozen out from this sea. Many feel isolated and are unaware of their oneness with the foundation. The perfection of wisdom is a time-honored practice for sentient beings to realize oneness with Universal Consciousness, which is boundless and benevolent. When beings merge into this foundation they automatically feel "greatly free and comfortable" (*dà zì-zài* 大自在) and are naturally imbued with "great mercy" (*dà cí-bēi* 大慈悲). Therefore they transcend all pain and suffering and dedicate themselves to helping those who are in distress.

Prajnaparamita

The Heart Sutra teaches that one can realize one's unrestrained and comfortable ground of existence by practicing the perfection of wisdom. "The perfection of wisdom" is translated from the Sanskrit term *prajnaparamita* (*bō-rě bō-luó-mì duō* 般若波羅蜜多), a combination of the word *prajna* (*bō-rě* 般若), which means wisdom, and the word *paramita* (*bō-luó-mì duō* 波羅蜜多), which refers to perfection or what has gone beyond. Hence, *prajnaparamita* may mean "the perfection of wisdom" or "wisdom of the beyond." Buddhism teaches that life is like a sea, at this shore of the sea is the realm of samsara (birth and death) and at the other shore, the beyond, is the realm of nirvana (free from birth and death). Sentient beings at this shore of samsara are usually ignorant and may fall into inverted delusions, whereas those who have reached the other shore of nirvana are enlightened, and are far away from inverted delusions.[12]

Metaphorically Gautama Buddha has gone to the beyond, and yet kindly stays at this shore providing rafts (expedient means) for the multitude to cross the sea of life from this shore to the beyond. He teaches six *paramitas*, six means to perfection, to the beyond. They are 1) *dana* (charity, bù-shī 布施), 2) *sila* (moral discipline, chí-jiè 持戒), 3) *kshanti* (endurance, rěn-rǔ 忍辱), 4) *virya* (zeal and habit, jīng-jìn 精進), 5) *dhyana* (meditation, chán-dìng 禪定), 6) *prajna* (wisdom, bō-rě 般若). In general, the practice of the perfection of wisdom implies the practice of all six perfections. Especially it is through meditation that one realizes the true essence of wisdom.[13]

Recall that one of the meanings of the term *bodhi* is perfect wisdom. Hence, we may say that the practice of the perfection of wisdom is to realize the nature of bodhi (or buddha nature), which is our comfortably unrestrained and benevolent ground of existence. In Buddhism, this practice is considered supreme and is extensively illumined in a great volume of six hundred scriptures called *The Prajnaparamita Sutras*. *The Heart Sutra*, which is a distillation of that great volume, teaches concisely how one can realize one's inherent buddha nature.

---

12 For more about inverted delusions, see chapter 4, pp. 53–54.
13 See the section "Zen Buddhism," chapter 3.

Chapter 1

Light Is Empty

When Bodhisattva Avalokitesvara is absorbed in deep meditation on the wisdom of the beyond, his *spiritual* eye beholds his ground of existence full of light with nothing in it. In that suprasensory state, he perceives the empty nature of the five aggregates: form, feeling, thinking, willing, and discerning.

Other religious traditions also mention the vision of light during deep meditation. We are to review a few ancient and modern writings to deepen our understanding of this divine experience.[14]

We first explore whether we can see pure light with our physical eyes. Physics Professor Arthur Zajonc remarks that he and a friend have constructed a science exhibit with a box containing a region filled with light. When experimenters look through a hole of the box into this region of light, they see complete darkness. However, when a wand specially placed outside the box is moved into the region, the wand appears brilliantly lit.[15] From this experiment, we deduce that our physical eyes do not see pure light, but only objects shone by light. Indeed, this experiment confirms a comment on the vision of light by Rudolf Steiner (1861–1925): "Many of us believe that we see light with our physical eyes. That is not correct. We do not see light, but only illuminated bodies. We do not see light, but we see through light."[16] Therefore, light is empty and our *physical* eyes do not see its pure form, but only see its commingled appearance of brightness and darkness.

Using the Taoists terms of *yin* and *yang*, we may say that our physical eyes do not see the pure yang aspect of light, except for

---

14 I have also surveyed this theme in my other book, *The Lord's Prayer: An Eastern Perspective*, chapter 1.

15 Zajonc, *Catching the Light*, p. 2. Recently I chanced upon this exhibit's other collaborator Mark Gardner, who graciously showed it to me in its storage area. However, he could not demonstrate its effects because there was not enough time to set up the experiment.

16 Steiner, *Manifestations of Karma*, p. 219.

its commingled appearances of yin and yang. However, those who have a well-formed *spiritual* eye (also called the "third eye," located between the eyebrows) can see the pure yang aspect of light. This pure light, which is not seen by physical eyes in the material world, is often referred to as "inner light."

To see inner light, Taoists practice regular meditation to develop the spiritual eye. A Taoist who is able to constantly stabilize a vision of inner light is said to have achieved eternal life—equivalently to have realized buddha nature by a Buddhist—and is referred to as a *real being* (zhēn-rén 真人) or an *immortal* (shén-xiān 神仙). For instance, the eight immortals of the Tang and Song Dynasties (618–1279) are well known in China. The legend of the eight immortals crossing a sea showing their divine power is a favorite folk art subject (see illustration). In the picture, all carry a special magical object that they use to bestow help and blessing. The man sitting at the leftmost with a sword at his back is their leader Lǚ Dòngbīn 呂洞賓 (b. 796). Lǚ is highly venerated and his teachings are compiled in a scripture called *The Secrets of the Golden Flower*.

The Eight Immortals Crossing a Sea

The Golden-Flower is a symbol for inner light. Let us look at the Chinese characters for Gold, Flower, and Light in the figure on the facing page. When we partly superimpose the character for Gold: 金 over the character for Flower: 花, we can discern the character

Chapter 1

Golden Flower as Inner Light

for Light: 光, hidden within. So, the *Golden-Flower* is a symbol for inner light. That Lǔ Dòngbīn nicknamed himself "Pure-yang-fellow" (*Chún-yáng-zi* 純陽子) clearly indicated his ability to constantly stabilize a vision of inner light.

Tibetan Buddhists refer to inner light as clear light. The Dalai Lama (b. Tenzin Gyatso, 1935) says that a gross form of clear light will arise briefly under the following four occasions in ordinary life: yawning, sneezing, the very moment of falling asleep or fainting, and the moment of sexual climax. He further indicates that meditation can stabilize the clear light when it arises and that in certain occult practices practitioners invoke sexual imageries as an aid to prolong their experience of clear light and to enhance its vividness.[17]

Not only Eastern religious traditions discuss inner light; Western scriptures also refer to this inner light. For example, the Gospel of John 1:1–4 says, "In the beginning was the Word, and the Word was with God, and the Word was God. He was with God in the beginning. Through him all things were made; without him nothing was made that has been made. *In him was life, and that life was the light of all humankind*" (italics added). According to St. John, through creation, the divine life in the Word became the inner light of human beings.

In the Gospel of Matthew 6:22, Jesus tells people when they may see this inner light, "If your eye is sound, your whole body will be full of light." A *sound eye* means a well-formed spiritual eye. Jesus

---

17 Hayward and Varela, *Gentle Bridges: Conversations with The Dalai Lama on the Sciences of Mind*, p. 81.

indicates that when the spiritual eye is fully developed, we can see our body full of inner light.

St. Teresa of Avila (1515–1582), a Spanish nun noted for her contemplative life, had certainly developed a sound eye to see inner light. She wrote, "...while the light we see here and the other light are both light, there is no comparison between the two and the brightness of the Sun seems quite dull if compared with the other."[18]

From these surveys we learn that meditation can help us develop the spiritual eye. Furthermore, when it becomes fully formed we can see our body consisting of nothing else except pure light, just as Bodhisattva Avalokita did while absorbed in the deep wisdom of the beyond.

Rudolf Steiner uses the term *suprasensory world* for what Buddhists refer to as "the beyond." He says that those (albeit very few) upon entering the suprasensory learn of three things: "the unmanifest light, the unspoken word, and the consciousness without knowledge of an object."[19]

So esotericism teaches that Universal Consciousness, the ground of our existence, consists of the unspoken word, the unmanifest light, and the consciousness without knowledge of an object. Avalokitesvara's report on meditation using the process of hearing and reflecting, concentrates on the unspoken word aspect. The statement: "Bodhisattva Avalokitesvara, while absorbed in the profundity of the perfection of wisdom, illuminated the five aggregates, and beheld them all empty" deals with the attributes of the unmanifest light and the consciousness without knowledge of an object. The rest of *The Heart Sutra* continues to expand on these two attributes more fully.

---

18 Teresa of Avila, *The Life of Teresa of Jesus*, ch. 38.
19 Steiner, *Man in the Light of Occultism, Theosophy and Philosophy*, lect. 2.

Chapter 2

舍利子, 色不異空, 空不異色, 色即是空, 空即是色, 受想行識, 亦復如是。

Listen, Sariputra, form is no different from emptiness, and emptiness is no different from form. Whatever is form is emptiness, and whatever is emptiness is form. The same holds for feeling, thinking, willing, and discerning.

Sariputra

Sariputra (*Shè-lì-zi* 舍利子), one of Gautama Buddha's ten principal disciples, is renowned for his supreme wisdom. It is natural that Bodhisattva Avalokita explained to him the practice of the perfection of wisdom. However, the longer version of *The Heart Sutra*[1] says that Sariputra asks Avalokitesvara the following question, "How should children of good families, who want to perform the practice of the profound perfection of wisdom, go forward?"[2] Since Sariputra engages Avalokitesvara in this dialogue for the sake of all future spiritual seekers who want to perform this practice, we may consider that Avalokitesvara is addressing to those for whom Sariputra is a stand-in.

We note with interest that Sariputra is related to two Buddhist items: *sarira* and *sarika*, both of which are also translated as *shè-lì* 舍利. *Sarira*s commonly refer to the pearl or crystal-like bead-shaped objects that are found among the cremated ashes of

---

1 See in the introduction about the difference between this short version and the longer one.
2 See for instance, Sonam, *The Heart Sutra: An Oral Teaching by Geshe Sonam Rinchen*, p. 35.

Sarira of Holy Sariputra from the collection of Chikai (Lobsang Khechok). Chikai, a Buddhist monk from Singapore and the owner of this sarira, told me that his collection of sariras was given to him mainly by an elderly Thai monk. He and the monk had "been practicing Dharma together for a long time." His whole collection is on view in his blog, mylotuspath.com/search/label/Sarira?m=0.

Buddhist saints,[3] and *sarika* is a small talking bird with clever and bright eyes.[4] Sariputra's mother was called *Sarika* because her eyes were clever and bright like that of a sarika. Incidentally a sample of the *sariras* that were left by Holy Sariputra looks like a lustrous pearl—reminiscent of a *sarika's* bright eye (see photo above).

---

3   We suspect that *sariras* are what the Rosicrucians called the "philosopher's stone" (the stone of the wise). Steiner explains that Rosicrucian initiates prepare the philosopher's stone through special breathing rhythms (which they learn privately from their teachers). Through this occult practice, the practitioners can cause the breathed-in oxygen to purify the carbons in their body instead of burning them into carbon dioxide (see, for instance, *Supersensible Knowledge,* lect. 11). Since Buddhist saints generally regulate their breath rhythms during meditation, it should be reasonable to find purified carbons, like pearls or crystal beads, in the remains of their cremated ashes.

4   See Soothill and Hodous, *A Dictionary of Chinese Buddhist Terms with Sanskrit and English Equivalents and a Sanskrit-Pali Index,* p. 278b.

Chapter 2

Undoubtedly, Sariputra was a devoted practitioner of the perfection of wisdom. However, in this commentary, we designate Sariputra as a representative of all aspiring spiritual practitioners of this practice rather than the historical personality. Kumarajiva 鳩摩羅什 and Xuánzàng 玄奘 had probably employed much deliberation in translating Sariputra as *Shè-lì-zi* 舍利子. It turns out that we can use his translated Chinese name to demonstrate the three phases of spiritual advancement in the practice of the perfection of wisdom. Such an interpretation of the translation may be unconventional. It nonetheless promotes a more critical reading of this scripture.

To begin with, the word *shè* 舍 may mean a dwelling as a noun or to give up as a verb. The word *lì* 利 connotes different meanings in different contexts, and here we take *lì* 利 to mean *profit* (*lì-yì* 利益), this being the most suitable for our present discussion. We shall introduce other meanings later. The word *zi* 子 is a courteous reference to a person. Thus, *Shè-lì-zi* 舍利子, the translation for Sariputra, may represent either those who keep profits in their dwelling or those who give up their profits.

By "those who keep profits in their dwelling," it is meant either literally those who hoard piles of material gains in their home or figuratively those who harbor the desire to amass material gains. Similarly, by "those who give up their profits," it is meant either literally those who cede their material gains or figuratively those who shun the desire for material gains.

When practitioners embark on the path of the perfection of wisdom, probably they are still entrapped in the sense perceptions of the material world and chained by the habitual urges "to keep profits in their dwelling." However, after they have learned the empty nature of the five aggregates: form, feeling, thinking, willing, and discerning, they gradually understand that material gains are not only irrelevant to their spiritual advancement, but on the contrary may be an obstacle to their realization of the clear and pure buddha nature. Thus, they willingly "give up their profits." In short, during the first phase of this practice, these spiritual seekers instill in themselves the habit of transforming from those *Shè-lì-zi* 舍利子 who keep profits in their dwelling to those *Shè-lì-zi* 舍利子 who give up their profits.

Form and Emptiness

When Bodhisattva Avalokitesvara is absorbed in deep meditation on the wisdom of the beyond, inner (clear) light arises. In that suprasensory state, he perceives the empty nature of the five aggregates: form, feeling, thinking, willing, and discerning. He feels free and comfortable (*zì-yóu-zì-zài* 自由自在), transcending all pain and suffering. Understandably, beginning spiritual aspirants as represented by Sariputra are far from such a blissful state. They most likely are still enmeshed in the physical world and regard all physical experiences as reality. So Avalokitesvara gives them a wake-up call and exhorts them to listen carefully:

> Listen, Sariputra, form is no different from emptiness, and emptiness is no different from form. Whatever is form is emptiness and whatever is emptiness is form. The same holds for feeling, thinking, willing, and discerning.

Of the five aggregates, form is directly related to matter, while the other four are mental activities associated with the mind. Thus it is easy to accept the emptiness of the four mental activities, but harder to agree to the emptiness of form. Buddhism explains that matter is the manifested form of the four great elements: earth, water, air, and fire, which are not real substances but are sensory qualities.[5] Considering this information, we delve into other cultural traditions to acquaint ourselves further with the relationship of "form and emptiness."

---

5   Section 4 of the appendix describes how the four great elements are created.

Chapter 2

Essence and Nothingness

First, let us review what Laozi says about essence (*yǒu* 有) and nothingness (*wú* 無), these two profound attributes of *Tao*:

> Nothingness is named for the origin of all things. Essence is named for the mother of all things.... These two [(essence and nothingness)] appear together. They differ in name, yet are considered the same. (無，名萬物之始也。有，名萬物之母也。...【有無】兩者同出，異名同謂。)[6]

Laozi states that these two attributes of *Tao* are like the two sides of a coin, always coexistent. *Tao* is at the same time showing in essence and vanishing in nothingness. In other words, *Tao* is always simultaneously revealing and unrevealing, concurrently producing and destroying.

The terms *essence* and *nothingness* and the terms *form* and *emptiness* essentially signify similar ideas. Suppose, in Avalokitesvara's statement, we replace *form* with *essence,* and *emptiness* with *nothingness*; and conversely, in Laozi's assertion, we reverse the substitutions. Then we shall see that the basic themes of these two lines remain intact:

> *Essence* is no different from *nothingness*, and *nothingness* is no different from *essence*. Whatever is *essence* is *nothingness* and whatever is *nothingness* is *essence*. (有不異無，無不異有，有即是無，無即是有。)

> *Emptiness* is named for the origin of all things. *Form* is named for the mother of all things.... These two [(*form* and *emptiness*)] appear together. They differ in name, yet are considered the same. (空，名萬物之始也。色，名萬物之母也。...【色空】兩者同出，異名同謂。)

---

6   *The Tao Te Ching*, ch. 1. The terms *essence and nothingness* (*yǒu-wú* 有無) are not in the original text, but are clearly implied in it; see Sit, *Lao Tzu and Anthroposophy*, ch. 1.

The preceeding exchanges show that writings in Buddhism and Taoism may use different terminologies; they fundamentally teach the same attributes of reality. Here, from *The Tao Te Ching*, we learn that form and emptiness may differ in name, yet are considered the same. Furthermore, they always appear together.

Sierpinski Triangle

Next, we inspect the modern fractal figure of the Sierpinski triangle to see how form and emptiness appear together. The Sierpinski triangle, which consists of patterns with progressively diminishing self-similar triangles, is an excellent model to illustrate the principle "as above, so below." Our main interest here is not to study this principle, but to explore the coexistence of form and emptiness of this figure. Here, we study a method (among many others) on how to construct the Sierpinski triangle that best demonstrates the relationship of form and emptiness as presented in *The Heart Sutra*.

To begin with, we take a blank triangle and join the mid points of its three sides. This initial step divides the blank triangle into four regions—an inner upside-down triangle and three outer upright triangles. Then, we divide each of the three upright triangles into four regions as in the first step, but keeping the upside-down triangle undivided.

We continue this process of either dividing all the upright triangles into four regions or keeping the upside-down triangles undivided ad infinitum. After enough steps, the Sierpinski triangle will take shape as shown. It consists of a central blank triangle and three outer triangles each of which has a pattern like the whole figure—this self-similar pattern is a typical feature of the principle "as above, so below."

Symbolically we may regard the blank space as the unrevealing attribute of Intelligence in the Absolute—the unspoken word, the unmanifest light, the consciousness without knowledge of an

Chapter 2

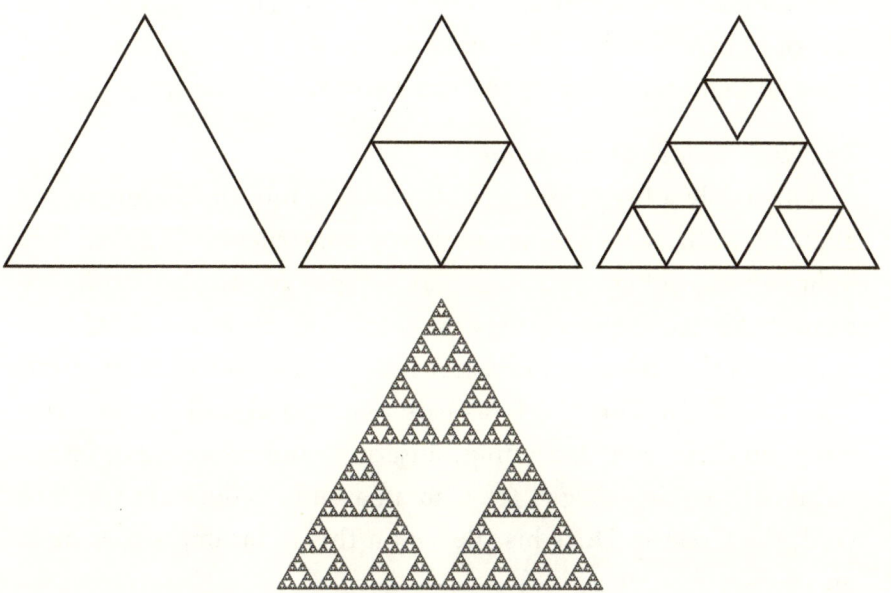

Sierpinski Triangle

object—and the pattern (form) as the revealing attribute of Intelligence in the physical world. The form is created in the empty space and the empty space lets form appear. Within the form, there is imbedded empty space. Form and emptiness commingle harmoniously. Thus, this figure clearly reflects the statement: "form is no different from emptiness; emptiness is no different from form. Whatever is form is emptiness, whatever is emptiness is form." Here, this statement is chiefly about the revealing attribute of Intelligence, rather than about the unrevealing Absolute.

Moreover, we may consider the central triangle as the core of human existence in pure yang and the three outer triangles as the physical appearances in a mixture of yin and yang. People with clairvoyance can behold the core in its empty essence as (inner, or clear) light and the outer appearances as light changing from emptiness to form and at the same time from form to emptiness continuously. Nonetheless, those with ordinary physical vision can only perceive the outer appearances as a *rigid* expression of form and emptiness rather than as a constant becoming.

Buddha's Silence on Creation

Obviously a blank triangle cannot turn into the Sierpinski triangle by itself; someone has to do the construction. Analogously light, which is of empty nature, cannot give rise to physical forms by itself; someone has to effect the transition. However, Buddhism maintains that there is no creator but only dependent origination (*yuán-qǐ* 缘起). This thesis asserts that things and events arise owing to their inter-depending causations and hence are of immaterial nature (*xìng-kōng* 性空). Gautama Buddha does not speak of God, the Creator. Does his silence on this point imply that he is an atheist?

I once related that the Indian mystic Sri Ramakrishna (1836–1886) discusses with his disciples why people mistake Gautama Buddha as an atheist. He tells them that Gautama Buddha "could not explain in words what he had realized by his *tapasya* (religious austerity)." The Buddha keeps silent about his inner experience and does not speak about God. So people mistake him to be an atheist. Sri Ramakrishna explains that the term *buddha* means one who becomes Intelligence itself. Essentially, Intelligence is what people refer to as God. In this respect, Gautama Buddha is not an atheist.[7]

Owing to his religious austerity, the Buddha remains silent to fourteen questions relating to cosmic and human relationships.[8] There is a deeper historical reason why the Buddha remains silent to those questions. Steiner observes that Gautama Buddha knows that his enlightenment experiences would be inaccessible to people's

---

7 See Sit, *The Lord's Prayer: An Eastern Perspective*, pp. 1–2; see also M., *The Gospel of Sri Ramakrishna*, p. 947.

8 See for instance, *The Buddha's Unanswerable Questions*, www.buddhists.livejournal.com/2844718.html.

ordinary faculty of vision in his time and the near future.[9] Hence, Gautama Buddha refrains from speaking of the fruits of his own enlightenment, but only formulates his teachings "to allow the human souls who receive them to become better and better."[10]

Gautama Buddha often says that the ultimate reality cannot be taught but has to be personally realized and thus it is necessary to differentiate between reality and the teachings on reality. *The Diamond Sutra* (*Jīn-gāng Jīng* 金剛經) is a famous exposition on this theme:

> The reality that the Tathagata has spoken cannot be grasped nor talked about, is neither the reality nor not the reality. (如來所說法, 皆不可取, 不可說, 非法, 非非法。) (ibid., ch. 7)
>
> That which is called the Buddha's teaching is not the Buddha's teaching. (所謂佛法者, 即非佛法。) (ibid., ch. 8)
>
> As to speaking reality, no reality can be spoken. Thus it is called "speaking reality." (說法者, 無法可說, 是名說法。) (ibid., ch. 21)

One of the difficulties in talking about reality is that reality is not rigid; it is something that is a constant becoming. In reality, producing and destroying occur jointly. Just as Laozi asserts, "These two appear together. They differ in name, yet are considered the same." Forms are created and dissolved concurrently. Only our eyes do not differentiate the moment we see something and the moment we realize we have seen something with a mental image. The mental image is no longer that something anymore, because that something has already disappeared and reappears—even its outer form seems the

---

[9] Steiner, *According to Luke*, p. 62. In the introduction I report that people lost clairvoyance at that time and that they focused on developing the mind soul for the next two millennia.

[10] Ibid., p. 104. The Buddha teaches the Eightfold Path (*Bā-zhèng-dào* 八正道; see chapter 3) to help people develop virtue and morality.

same. Therefore, once the reality has been described, the description becomes rigid and what is said is not the reality anymore.[11]

In the beginning line of *The Tao Te Ching*, Laozi captures this aspect of reality concisely: "The *Tao* that can be spoken is not the eternal *Tao*" (道可道也，非恆道也).[12] This may be the reason that the Chinese classic *Book of Changes* (*Yi Jīng* 易經) utilizes symbolic hexagrams to illustrate the continuous changing attribute of reality. As for the Buddha, he speaks in oxymoron to convey this mysterious aspect of reality.

Higher Beings Create Forms in Light

Since the time of Gautama Buddha, human consciousness has much progressed. People have fully developed their mind to reason logically and are ready to cultivate intellectually clear clairvoyance to view the spiritual world. Now people will again be able to access Buddha's enlightenment.

The great spiritual teacher Rudolf Steiner reintroduces cosmic knowledge into human consciousness, thus paving a way for humankind to reconnect with the spiritual world. In his autobiography, he explains, "When we perceive the world through our senses, we see an illusion. But when we add thinking that is free of the senses—from our own inner being—to sense perception, illusion is permeated with reality and ceases to be illusion."[13] Let us now dip into a few of his lectures to decipher the relationships of matter, form, and emptiness.

---

11 See, for example, Steiner, *A Way of Self-knowledge and the Threshold of the Spiritual World,* especially part 1.

12 This statement lends itself to many interpretations. I once rendered it as: "A *Tao* that can be a road is not the eternal *Tao*." Please see comments about the meanings of the word *Tao* 道 in my book *Lao Tzu and Anthroposophy* (2nd ed.), pp. 3–4.

13 Steiner, *Autobiography*, p. 85. In *How to Know Higher Worlds,* Steiner presents many exercises that can help the mind to bring forth and stabilize sense-free thought.

Chapter 2

Every substance upon the Earth is condensed light.... Wherever you reach out and touch a substance, there you have condensed, compressed light. All matter is, in its essence, light.[14]

Everything in that physical world is maya, including our physical body. Through what, is this really there? Through what do the animals, plants and stones around us exist? Through the fact that higher beings took a thought many millions of years ago and thought it over and over again. In these things it's as the proverb says; steady dripping hollows the stone. The same thoughts cover each other and eventually form physical objects. The harder a stone is, the longer beings thought it. Our physical body is nothing else than the thought of many higher beings.[15]

When certain forms, created under the influence of the Spirits of Form,[16] reach a certain stage, they are shattered. And when you look at these broken forms, which arise when suprasensory forms are shattered, what you are seeing is the transition from suprasensory to the sense-perceptible aspect of space. That broken form is matter. When matter appears in the universe, for the person with spiritual vision, it is nothing other than smashed, shattered, exploded form.[17]

Recall that, earlier, we discussed how the dependent origination principal does not account adequately for the rise of forms from light. Here, we learn from Anthroposophy that those who have cultivated sense-free thinking can perceive that forms are the created thoughts of higher spiritual beings.

To summarize, we have explored the relationship of form and emptiness from the teachings in Buddhism, *The Tao Te Ching*,

---

14   Steiner, *Manifestations of Karma*, p. 188.
15   Steiner, *Esoteric Lessons 1910–1912*, Jan. 17, 1911, p. 109.
16   "Spirits of Form" are a certain rank of higher beings. Please refer to the appendix for more about the nine ranks of hierarchies and their creations.
17   Steiner, *The World of the Senses: And the World of the Spirit*, pp. 52–53.

fractal theory, and Anthroposophy. These teachings clarify the meaning of maya and deepen our appreciation of reality. We gradually understand why practitioners of the perfection of wisdom aspire to transform themselves from the *Shè-lì-zi* who keeps profits to the *Shè-lì-zi* who gives up profits. Their ideal is primarily the same as that of a Taoist: "Observe purity and embrace simplicity; diminish selfishness and minimize cravings" (見素抱樸, 少私寡欲).[18]

---

18   Laozi, *The Tao Te Ching*, chapter 19.

Chapter 3

舍利子，是諸法空相，不生不滅，不垢不淨，不增不減。是故空中無色，無受想行識，無眼耳鼻舌身意，無色聲香味觸法，無眼界，乃至無意識界。無無明，亦無無明盡，乃至無老死，亦無老死盡，無苦集滅道，無智亦無得。

> Here, Sariputra, all dharmas are a semblance of emptiness that is neither produced nor destroyed, neither defiled nor cleansed, and neither increased nor decreased. Therefore, in emptiness there is neither form, nor feeling, nor thinking, nor willing, nor discerning; neither eye, ear, nose, tongue, body, nor mind; neither form, sound, smell, taste, tactility, nor mental objects; neither a field of vision nor even a field of cognition. There is neither ignorance nor an end to ignorance, even neither aging and death nor an end to aging and death. There is no suffering, no cause of suffering, no extinction of suffering, and no path to an end of suffering. There is no knowledge and no attainment.

Dharma Negations

In Chapters 1 and 2, we learn that the Absolute is the unspoken word, the unmanifest light, and the consciousness without knowledge of an object and that the material world is in effect condensed forms of pure light. Hence, all *dharmas,* a Sanskrit term meaning laws of nature or that which support nature, are accordingly a semblance of emptiness. Emptiness, as the below reflecting the above, the Absolute, is eternal like the unspoken word, neither produced nor destroyed; is perfect like the unmanifest light, neither defiled nor cleansed; is complete like the consciousness without knowledge of an object, neither increased nor decreased. Since dharmas are only a semblance of emptiness, they have no intrinsic existence and only support the functions of maya.

We observe things in the physical world being produced and destroyed, being defiled and cleansed, and being increased and decreased. Nevertheless, we learn from *The Tao Te Ching* that in reality, the producing and the destroying are taking place concurrently; likewise, so are the defiling and the cleansing, the increasing and the decreasing. These physical phenomena are the profound attributes of Intelligence in the revealing state as symbolized by the three outer triangles of the Sierpinski triangle. The unrevealing Absolute as symbolized by the central triangle is unknowable by physical means. To know it is to experience it in spirit, to be at one with it, or in Buddhist terms, to realize the buddha nature.

The experience of reality is difficult to articulate and at best one can say what it is not. Therefore, Gautama Buddha says, "The reality that the Tathagata has spoken cannot be grasped nor talked about, is neither the reality nor not the reality" (see chapter 2). His teachings on how to realize reality are collected in a six hundred volume scripture called *The Prajnaparamita Sutras,* of which *The Heart Sutra* is a compendium. In this passage of *The Heart Sutra*, Bodhisattva Avalokita focuses on the empty characteristics of all dharmas.

Before speaking on the emptiness of all dharmas, Avalokitesvara calls on Sariputra's name again. This calling on his name signifies what Sariputra and those whom he represents are to accomplish in the second phase of this practice.

Recall from chapter 2:

> To begin with, the word *shè* 舍 may mean a dwelling as a noun or to give up as a verb. The word *lì* 利 connotes different meanings in different contexts, and here, we take *lì* 利 to mean *profit* (*lì-yì* 利益), this being the most suitable to our present discussion. We shall introduce other meanings later. The word *zi* 子 is a courteous reference to a person. Thus, *Shè-lì-zi* 舍利子, the translation for Sariputra, may represent either those who keep profits in their dwelling or those who give up their profits.

By "those who keep profits in their dwelling," it is meant either literally those who hoard piles of material gains in their home or figuratively those who harbor the desire to amass material gains. Similarly, by "those who give up their profits," it is meant either literally those who cede their material gains or figuratively those who shun the desire for material gains.

There we then explore why practitioners aspire to transform themselves from the *Shè-lì-zi* who keeps profits to the *Shè-lì-zi* who gives up profits.

Now we suggest another interpretation for the word *lì* 利, as in *biàn-lì* 便利, which translates literally as *expedient means* (convenience). Hence, the name *Shè-lì-zi* may stand for those who dwell on grasping all expedient means or those who let go of them. Buddhist teachings regard all dharmas simply as expedient means. In this second phase of practice, Bodhisattva Avalokita articulates that practitioners are to transform themselves from those *Shè-lì-zi* who hold onto all dharmas to those *Shè-lì-zi* who release all dharmas. We shall see how Avalokitesvara methodically leads them to loosen their tight grip of all the dharmas.

We learn that our ground of existence is intrinsically empty, and the laws that uphold our existence are consequently also empty of characteristic. Thus, what can be said about a subject of emptiness? Avalokitesvara uses a method which experienced teachers often employ when teaching a difficult subject. Instead of discussing the attributes of the subject, they discuss its opposite features. For, learning *what a subject isn't* may enhance knowing *what it is*. At this stage, Sariputra and those whom he represents are undoubtedly well versed with Gautama Buddha's early teachings. Thus, it would be easy for them to appreciate the empty nature of Intelligence by simply adding the word *wú* 無 ("no")[1] to every topic that they have previously learned. Therefore, Sariputra

---

1   In my translation, I use either the word *no* or the words *neither, nor* for *wú* 無.

and those whom he represents are to embark on a learning path "to learn unlearning."[2]

Early Buddhism

Let us briefly review Buddha's early teachings that are related to the topics in this passage of *The Heart Sutra*. Obviously early Buddhism is much broader than what is mentioned in this passage. This passage only focuses on the topics that practitioners of the perfection of wisdom have to consider for the *unlearning*.

Among these topics, we have already dealt with the empty nature of the five aggregates: form, feeling, thinking, willing, and discerning. Therefore, we now only discuss the rest. Buddhism teaches that people possess eight consciousnesses. The first five consciousnesses are for sensory perception: seeing, hearing, smelling, tasting, and touching. The sixth consciousness is for sense cognition—discerning. The seventh consciousness, called *klista-mano* (*mò-nà-shi* 末那識), is for pondering and calculating. It is this seventh consciousness that creates egoism and the idea of the self. This seventh submits all the sense experiences of the first six to the eighth consciousness *alaya-vijnana* (*ā-lài-yé-shi* 阿賴耶識), which is for storage of all life experiences. The first seven consciousnesses arise based on what is stored in the eighth.

Of these eight consciousnesses, the first six are related to the senses. In short, the sense instruments are called the *six-root* (*liù-gēn* 六根): eye, ear, nose, tongue, body, and mind. The objects sensed by the six sense instruments are called the *six-dust* (*liù-chén* 六塵): forms by eye, sounds by ear, smells by nose, tastes by tongue, tactilities by body, and mental objects by mind. The sense processes are referred to as the *six-element* (*liù-jiè* 六界), which includes the field of vision and the field of cognition.[3] Buddhist teachings also mention a term *eighteen-element* (*shí-bā-jiè* 十八界) in association with the

---

2 *Xué-bù-xué* 學不學, *The Tao Te Ching*, chapter 64.

3 Generally, these terms represent the range and direction to which the sense organs may reach during the sense process rather than the sense process

six senses. For instance, the sense of seeing comprises these three elements: eyes, objects seen, and the process of seeing. Thus there are altogether six times three (eighteen) elements related to the six senses.

Gautama Buddha expounded on this doctrine of sense consciousness more than two millennia ago. The modern Anthroposophy teacher Rudolf Steiner regards sense consciousness in a much broader scope and holds that each human being has a system of twelve senses, seven of which are for learning the outside environment and five for knowing the inner self. He explains,

> "I" sense, sense of thinking, word sense, sense of hearing, sense of warmth, sense of sight and sense of taste are outwardly directed senses. On the other hand, where we predominantly perceive ourselves through the things and where we perceive more the effects of things in us, we have the remaining senses: Life sense, sense of movement, sense of balance, and the senses of touch and smell.[4]

He adds that, in everyday life, We do not clearly perceive things that occur in the realm of the inwardly directed senses; they remain subconscious. We mainly perceive their effects on our inner being. For instance, the sense of life is the feeling of well-being, which is heightened after a good meal. We perceive whether or how we are in motion through the sense of movement. The sense of balance is a pure soul experience, making us feel as spirit with inner tranquility. It is through the sense of touch that we ascertain the existence of the outer world, which is "all-pervading substance of God" and lastly, people can have mystic union with God through the sense of smell.[5]

---

per se. Thus, these terms in the Buddhist context have a slightly broader meaning than their common usage.

4 Steiner, *Spiritual Science as a Foundation for Social Forms,* lect. 3 (tr. rev.).

5 Ibid. For information on how the twelve senses arise and work, refer to the first four lectures in Steiner, *A Psychology of Body, Soul, and Spirit.* See also a summary of the 12 senses and their relation with human organizations on page 42.

senses of cognition *nerve-sense organization*	sense of self ("I") sense of thinking sense of word sense of hearing
senses of feeling *rhythmic organization*	sense of warmth sense of sight sense of taste sense of smell
senses of will *metabolic-limb system*	sense of touch sense of balance sense of one's motion sense of being

As people live on Earth, they are aided by the senses. Yet, what draws people to be born on Earth? Buddhism teaches that there are twelve causes (*shí'-èr-yīn-yuán* 十二因緣) linking human existence on Earth. They are ignorance (*wú-míng* 無明), willing (*xíng* 行), discerning (*shi* 識), name and form (*míng-sè* 名色), six-sense (*liù-rù* 六入), contact (*chù* 觸), feeling (*shòu* 受), craving (*ài* 愛), grasping (*qǔ* 取), becoming (*yǒu* 有), birth (*shēng* 生), and aging and death (*lǎo-sǐ* 老死). The dependent origination principle explains how one cause links to the next, trapping human beings cyclically in the wheel of samsara (birth and death). If people systematically end these causes one after another, from the extinction of ignorance to the extinction of aging and death, then they will be free from the wheel of birth and death.

Gautama Buddha observes that people on Earth suffer from illness, aging, and death. To help them liberate themselves from such suffering, he teaches the Four Noble Truths (*Sì-Shèng-Dì* 四聖諦): the knowledge of suffering (*kǔ* 苦), the knowledge of the causes of suffering (*jí* 集), the knowledge of the necessity for liberation from suffering (*miè* 滅), and, lastly, the knowledge of the means of liberation from suffering (*dào* 道). He further teaches people to practice the Eightfold Path (*Bā-Zhèng-Dào* 八正道)—listed below—to develop virtue and morality. Those who diligently practice the Eightfold Path can eventually end the twelve causes linking human existence on Earth, attain liberation from the cycle of birth and death, and thus suffer no more.

The Eightfold Path

1. Right View   (*Zhèng-Jiàn* 正見)
2. Right Intention   (*Zhèng-Sī* 正思)
3. Right Speech   (*Zhèng-Yǔ* 正語)
4. Right Action   (*Zhèng-Yè* 正業)
5. Right Career   (*Zhèng-Mìng* 正命)
6. Right Zeal and Habit (*Zhèng-Jīng-Jìn* 正精進)
7. Right Memory   (*Zhèng-Niàn* 正念)
8. Right Meditation   (*Zhèng-Dìng* 正定)[6]

This brief account constitutes the main tenets of Buddha's early teachings. According to Buddhist tradition, different groups of sixteen, eighteen, and five hundred disciples of Gautama Buddha had attained the liberation from the cycle of samsara (birth and death). These saints are called arhats (*à-luó-hàn* 阿羅漢) and the historical Sariputra was revered as a highly accomplished arhat.[7]

---

[6] In *How to Know Higher Worlds*, Steiner indicates that the development of the spiritual organs are related to the sixteen-petal lotus flower (also called sixteen-spoke chakra) near the larynx and the twelve-petal lotus flower (twelve-spoke chakra) near the heart. Half of the petals in these two lotus flowers had been developed in the distant past but were then laid dormant. The other remaining petals are still to be developed. Nowadays, spiritual seekers who engage in esoteric practice can develop these other petals and make the dormant ones active again. Steiner says that the conscientious practice of the Eightfold Path is conducive to the development of the eight undeveloped petals in the sixteen-petal lotus flower (ibid., pp. 112–118).

[7] See *Arhat (Buddhism)*, "In Mahayana Buddhism": www.en.wikipedia.org/wiki/Arhat_(Buddhism)#In_Mah.C4.81y.C4.81na_Buddhism.

Later, Gautama Buddha teaches the practice of the bodhisattva path, the way of complete enlightenment for the benefit of all sentient beings. This school of knowledge, which centers on the practice of the perfection of wisdom, is referred to as Mahayana Buddhism. Mahayana means the "great vehicle" and is an honorary reference to the practice of bodhisattvas. The practice for self-liberation from the cycle of birth and death, is called *Hinayana* ("small vehicle"). This practice of the early teachings is also preferably called *Theravada* ("teachings of the elders"). Certain Buddhist scholars opine that the historical Sariputra might not have fully mastered the essence of Mahayana Buddhism. So Gautama Buddha inspired him to ask Avalokitesvara about how to practice the perfection of wisdom.

Since the practice of the perfection of wisdom is to know reality, to realize buddha nature for the benefit of all sentient beings, the teachings that concern the liberation from the cycle of birth and death become irrelevant. Therefore, in imparting this supreme teaching, Bodhisattva Avalokita adds the word *wú* 無 ("no") to the aforementioned topics. These negations are not meant to deny the validity of the early teachings of the Buddha, but to highlight their futility in the practice of Mahayana Buddhism.

Zen Buddhism

Zen Buddhism is noted for its practice of Mahayana Buddhism. The First Patriarch of Zen Bodhidharma (*Pútí-dá-mó* 菩提達摩; c. fifth century), who came to China from India, centered his practice and teachings on meditation and on *The Lankavatara Sutra* (*Léng-jiā Jīng* 楞伽經). Later on, Zen masters encouraged students to also study *The Diamond Sutra*.

The object of Zen is to realize buddha nature through meditation. The story of how the Fifth Patriarch of Zen Hóngrěn 弘忍 (601–675) selected his successor exemplifies cogently the essential teachings of Zen. The Sixth Patriarch of Zen Huìnéng 惠能 (638–713) told the story himself. Here, we briefly present the relevant points of this anecdote and then in chapter 5 we shall relate in greater detail the enlightenment story of Huìnéng.

The Fifth Patriarch told monks in his monastery to write a poem about meditation so that he could determine who might succeed him. The head monk Shénxiù 神秀 (c. 606–706) wrote:

> The body is a bodhi tree; 身是菩提樹
> The mind a clear mirror stand be. 心如明鏡台
> And wipe it oft with great respect, 時時勤拂拭
> Not letting any dust collect. 勿使惹塵埃

Then Huìnéng, a junior monk who was just a kitchen helper at the time, wrote,

> By nature, bodhi is no tree; 菩提本無樹
> Nor the clear mirror a stand be. 明鏡亦非台
> Nothing e'er exists in effect; 本來無一物
> In which place can dust collect? 何處惹塵埃 [8]

After reading the poems, the Fifth Patriarch knew that the young monk Huìnéng understood the empty nature of bodhi while the head monk Shénxiù did not. Therefore, he promoted Huìnéng to be the Sixth Patriarch.[9]

From this story we see that the proper view of "emptiness" plays a very important role in the Zen tradition. Moreover, when imparting the dharma on buddha nature, the early Zen masters exercised great care and caution. Whenever possible, they refrained from mentioning the term *buddha nature* and used a word such as *thusness* or *suchness* instead, and some even used only a finger pointing to the

---

8   This poem is widely known. However, a recently discovered Dūnhuáng 敦煌 edition reads a little differently: "By nature, bodhi is no tree; / Nor the clear mirror a stand be. / Buddha nature is always clean; / In which place can dust be seen?" (菩提本無樹, 明鏡亦無台; 佛姓常清淨, 何處有塵埃). See for instance, www.baike.com/wiki/旅顺博物馆藏敦煌本六祖坛经.

9   *The Platform Sutra of the Sixth Patriarch*, ch. 1 (paraphrased).

empty space to symbolize the emptiness of reality. Though buddha nature is universal among all people, its realization is a rather personal experience. Teachers may discern whether a student is ready to realize buddha nature as in the case of Huìnéng and Shénxiù; however they cannot teach enlightenment routinely. Moreover, teachers do not particularly urge students to seek enlightenment for fear of an opposite effect delaying them from attaining enlightenment.

I call this opposite effect in fulfilling one's desire the *persist–resist* principle.[10] When we persist in wanting to get something, be it physical or spiritual, it will resist in appearing to us. Once we relinquish the want, the item will soon appear. For example, many of us probably have experienced frustration in not being able to find, say, a misplaced key. Just when we give up the search, we will then fortuitously notice the key lying somewhere.

Essentially the *persist–resist* principle is to remind people "not to dwell on anything when activating the mind" (應無所住而生其心).[11] Therefore, Zen masters refrain from urging students to realize buddha nature, and instead they use favorable situations to guide their students to experience the reality themselves.

All students (indeed all human beings) have buddha nature. However, most of them are unaware, and unwittingly keep searching for it. In Zen tradition, these students are compared to people who forget that they have a lamp in their hand and keep looking for it. Their teachers wait for a suitable moment to point out the obvious incongruity. The stories of Zen masters, and especially the enlightenment anecdotes of their students, were frequently recorded. For instance, the volume *The Records of the Transmission of the Lamp* (*Jǐng-dé Chuán Dēng Lù* 景德傳燈錄) is full of such documents. In Zen tradition, these records are referred to as *koans* (*gōng'-àn* 公

---

10 To learn more about this principle, see Sit, *The Lord's Prayer,* pp. 88–93, and *Lao Tzu and Anthroposophy,* pp. 50–52.

11 *The Diamond Sutra,* ch. 10.

案). *The Gateless Pass of Zen* (*Chán-zōng Wú Mén Guān* 禪宗無門關), which enjoys a wide readership both in the East and the West, is a thin book of forty-eight intriguing koans.

As a means to enlightenment, Zen teachers of later periods would suggest their students either to meditate on a koan (*cān gōng'-àn* 參公案), or to meditate on a pivoting word or phrase of a koan (*cān huà-tóu* 參話頭). During the Song Dynasty (c. 950–1300) this form of meditation became very popular and it gradually turned into a formal Zen practice, which lasts to this day.

Calligraphy of The Heart Sutra

In the introduction, I mention a copy of *The Heart Sutra* in Chinese calligraphy by the well-known calligrapher Ōuyáng Xún 歐陽詢 (557–641). During the writing of this book, I learned that Ōuyáng Xún could not himself have produced it. Someone else must have forged the piece by either imitating Ōuyáng's writing style or collaging Ōuyáng's various calligraphic works. We shall examine the background related to this faked item and hence deduce that it is more likely an imitation than a collage.

Even though the piece shows the name of Ōuyáng Xún in the heading and on the last line, it was not created by Ōuyáng Xún for the following two conspicuous reasons. First, the version of *The Heart Sutra* as shown in the calligraphy was not available for Ōuyáng Xún during his lifetime. It is known that Xuánzàng 玄奘 (602–664) studied Buddhism in India for about sixteen years, returned to China in 645, and translated this sutra in 649 (see the introduction). However, Ōuyáng Xún passed away in 641, four years before the return of Xuánzàng and eight years before the translation of this sutra. Second, in the calligraphy—see the illustration on page 48—the beginning four characters in the leftmost line, 貞觀九年 (*Zhēnguàn jiǔ-nián*) mean that the calligraphy was done in 635, when Xuánzàng was still in India. These discrepancies clearly indicate that the piece was a fake created at the earliest in 645 (when Xuánzàng was back in China), but most likely in or after 649 (when this translation was readily available).

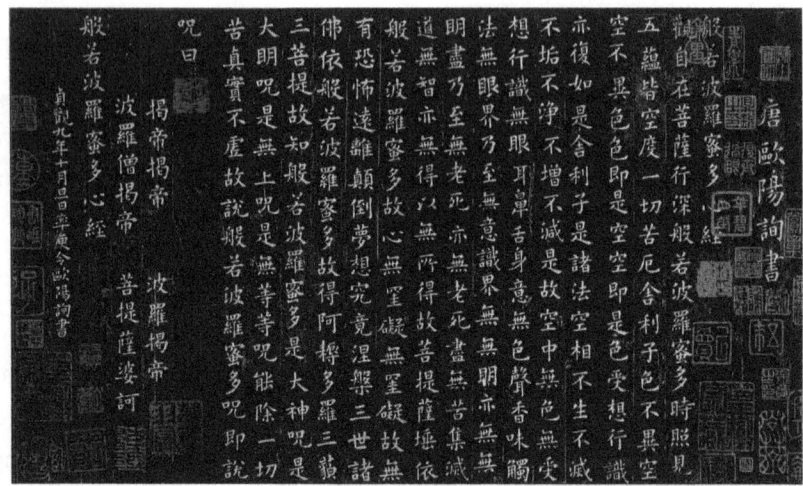

Calligraphy of The Heart Sutra

Now, as these facts can be openly checked from historical documents, we wonder why someone would take the trouble to forge an item with such a glaring discrepancy. If this individual were making forgery art objects for profit, he could have picked a piece of literary work that existed before 635 or he could have selected a calligrapher that was still alive after the translation of this sutra. Yet he chose to create a fake with a popular sutra in the style of a famous calligrapher whose death preceded its translation. He left this piece like a koan for readers to ponder.

I suspect that this unknown individual was an enlightened master who was well versed in the teachings of *The Heart Sutra*. He probably aimed to use the piece to illustrate the semblance of things. The forms (in this case, the calligraphic style and the name of the calligrapher) of the work appear to be that of Ōuyáng Xún. Yet if people are not deluded by these forms and investigate, they will discover the truth. For this purpose, a simple imitation rather than an elaborate collage of calligraphic works is sufficient. The piece can serve as a vehicle to teach that in the world of maya, what appears to be is really not, just as the body appears to be a bodhi tree but is not.

The Koan of Raising a Finger

Let us study a koan from *The Gateless Pass of Zen* to see how a Zen master named Jùzhī 俱胝 (c. ninth century) helped his student attain enlightenment.

> Jùzhī always imparted the dharma by raising a finger. One day, someone asked Jùzhī's boy attendant what essentially his master taught. This boy answered by raising a finger exactly as his master usually did. Later, when Jùzhī learned of this incident, he used a knife to cut off the boy's finger. The boy cried in pain and sped off. Jùzhī called him back. Just as the boy turned his head backward, Jùzhī raised a finger. Suddenly, the boy became enlightened.[12]

A koan is like an intricately cut diamond with many facets reflecting light. It can lend itself to many possible interpretations. Here we inspect a facet of this koan that aptly elucidates this passage of *The Heart Sutra*.

The koan says that the master always imparted the dharma by raising a finger. Conceivably mature spiritual seekers could understand that the gesture was a device showing the emptiness of reality. The master obviously knew his boy attendant was not yet mature enough to discern the true meaning of this gesture. Therefore, when he found out the innocent boy had imitated this gesture, he decided to shock the boy and awaken him to reality.

He did this by cutting off the boy's finger. The boy, feeling pain and angry, naturally sped away. Then he knew the boy would be shocked if he called him back. The shock would awaken the boy and

---

12 *The Gateless Pass of Zen,* third item (paraphrased). See www.baus-ebs.org/sutra/fan-read/oo3/o3-o16.htm for the Chinese text or www.sacred-texts.com/bud/glg/glgo3.htm for a translated version.

prepare him to receive the dharma. Thus when the boy turned his head after being called back, the master raised a finger to impart the dharma. The amazed boy suddenly became enlightened because his master had created a situation for him to recognize reality. Hence he got the insight that a finger has nothing to do with the dharma (else his finger would not have been cut off) and the proper view that in reality there is neither finger nor dharma but only emptiness.

Here, we may regard the negatives in this passage of *The Heart Sutra* as a symbolic knife. Avalokitesvara uses this knife of negativity to cut off a practitioner's grasping finger to release one's bondage to the dharmas. Thus, at the completion of the second phase of this practice, Sariputra and all those he represents will transform from the *Shè-lì-zi* who grasps expedient means to the *Shè-lì-zi* who lets go of expedient means. Henceforth, "They will hold the proper view that all supportive dharmas are like a dream, a phantom, a bubble, or a shadow, like a droplet of dew or a flash of lightning" (一切有為法，如夢幻泡影，如露亦如電，應作如是觀).[13]

---

13   *The Diamond Sutra*, ch. 32.

Chapter 4

以無所得故，菩提薩埵，依般若波羅蜜多故，心無罣礙，無罣礙故，無有恐怖，遠離顛倒夢想，究竟涅槃。三世諸佛，依般若波羅蜜多故，得阿耨多羅三藐三菩提。

> Without aiming for attainment, and only relying on the perfection of wisdom, bodhisattvas find no obstacles in the mind. With no obstacles, they have no fear. They depart afar from inverted delusions, and eventually enter nirvana. Relying on the perfection of wisdom, all buddhas in the Three Times fully awaken to the unexcelled-complete-universal-enlightenment.

The Bodhisattva Path

The last sentence of the previous passage of *The Heart Sutra* reads, "There is no knowledge and no attainment." By that it is meant that the knowledge of the Four Noble Truths (*Sì-Shèng-Dì* 四聖諦) for attaining liberation from the cycle of samsara (birth and death) is no longer relevant. Bodhisattvas who practice Mahayana Buddhism do not aim to gain liberation from birth and death—it does not mean that they do not practice the Eightfold Path (*Bā-Zhèng-Dào* 八正道), which is the base for inner development. They wholeheartedly purify themselves to clearly realize reality, the true nature of bodhi (perfect wisdom).

In this passage of *The Heart Sutra*, there is no mention of Sariputra since this phase of the practice is usually referred to as the bodhisattva path. Even so, we can still use the translation *Shè-lì-zi* 舍利子 to illustrate the advancement of the bodhisattvas. In chapters 2 and 3, we use *Shè-lì-zi* to present those practitioners who transform themselves from keeping profits (*lì-yì* 利益) to giving up profits, and then from grasping expedient means (*biàn-lì* 便利) to letting go of expedient means. Now, we share a third interpretation of the name *Shè-lì-zi* through another meaning of the word *lì* 利.

The word *lì* 利 can mean benefits (*fú-lì* 福利), which broadly encompass profits, conveniences, and blessings. The translated name *Shè-lì-zi* may stand either for those who dwell on attaining benefits or for those who relinquish benefits. In the first two phases of practice, practitioners mainly train the self to surrender material things and spiritual dharmas. Now, in the third phase of practice, they embark on the bodhisattva path, benefiting self to benefit others (*zì-lì-lì-tā* 自利利他). They practice all six *paramitas*, the first of which is the perfection of charity. (Ordinary charity is giving when being asked to give, whereas perfect charity is giving without being asked to give.) Awakening within, bodhisattvas automatically spread inner light abroad. They do not keep the gained blessings of inner light, but kindly endow them to others. Symbolically they become a light bearer in this world of maya, like what Jesus says, "Let your light so shine before men, that they may see your good works" (Matt. 5:16).

Tibetan Buddhism teaches a meditative practice called *tonglen* (taking and giving) in which one takes in people's pain and suffering during the in-breath and gives them joy and happiness during the out-breath. Obviously the breath helps people maintain their life. However, when one inhales pain and suffering and exhales joy and happiness, one is assuredly living for the benefit of others. So, in essence, *tonglen* is a practice of benefiting self to benefit others. The Tibetan Buddhist nun Pema Chödrön (b. 1938) observes that this practice can awaken one's heart and courage, and hence can generate great compassion toward others.[1] It is miraculous that pain and suffering can become fuel for the generation of courage and compassion.

---

1   Chödrön, *The Wisdom of No Escape*, pp. 57–64.

Chapter 4

Bodhisattva Avalokita indicates that the third phase of the practice of the perfection of wisdom is to go into the beyond.[2] Bodhisattvas purify themselves to clearly realize buddha nature step by step—fifty-two steps all together. Their mind progressively awakens with no obstacles. They understand that the revealing attribute of Intelligence is a constant becoming and the physical world is only illusion, maya. Hence, they have no fear to live in the physical world and dedicate themselves to helping others become enlightened. They depart afar from the inverted delusions and know that when entering nirvana they will experience "eternity, joy, the Self, and purity" (*cháng-lè-wǒ-jìng* 常樂我淨).

Concerning the meaning of "eternity, joy, the Self, and purity," Gautama Buddha observes that common people may commit four kinds of inverted delusions in two opposite directions. In one direction, some mistake illusion for reality and think of the impermanent as eternity (*wú-cháng-jì-cháng* 無常計常), suffering as joy (*kǔ-zhě-jì-lè* 苦者計樂), non-Self as the Self (*wú-wǒ-jì-wǒ* 無我計我), and defilement as purity (*bù-jìng-jì-jìng* 不淨計淨). In the other direction, some have learned that the physical world is maya, yet they practice erroneously and regard eternity as the impermanent (*cháng-jì-wú-cháng* 常計無常), joy as suffering (*lè-zhě-jì-kǔ* 樂者計苦), the Self as non-Self (*wǒ-jì-wú-wǒ* 我計無我), and purity as defilement (*jìng-jì-bù-jìng* 淨計不淨). He advises his monks not to cultivate the notion of the impermanent, suffering, non-Self, and defilement as reality, but constantly meditate upon the idea of "eternity, joy, the Self, and purity" as reality.[3]

---

2   Please note that the term *beyond* in this context does not signify a faraway place. The ground of human existence is Intelligence, or bodhi, which is not located in any particular place—neither inside the body nor outside the body. No word can express its whereabouts; *beyond* is just a provisional term.

3   See *The Mahaparinirvana Sutra* (*Dà Bānnièpán Jīng* 大般涅槃經), chapter 2 www.cbeta.org/result/normal/T12/0374_002.htm.

In other words, one type of unenlightened people mistake semblance for reality and seek only physical experiences; they certainly do not realize reality. Another type of unenlightened people understand that semblance is not reality but seek total annihilation; thus they also miss out on reality. Indeed, Anthroposophy teaches that there are two types of spiritual beings that lag behind, referred to collectively as Ahriman and Lucifer, whose impulses trap people in inverted delusions. The Ahrimanic forces lead people to believe that this physical world is the only reality and the Luciferic forces tempt people to forsake physical experiences and pursue only spirituality. Steiner says that when people recognize and strive to balance these forces they can transcend these delusions.[4]

With neither fear nor inverted delusions, bodhisattvas compassionately keep being incarnated on Earth to help others. They progressively become purer and more enlightened. Eventually at the completion of their path, they enter nirvana, the total dissolution of individual existence. They merge into Intelligence and yet they still retain their own personality.[5] They become a buddha and will not be born on Earth again.

Buddhas are those bodhisattvas who live their last incarnated life on Earth. Bodhisattva Avalokita notes that buddhas in the Three Times are not practicing any more advanced teachings. They also practice the perfection of wisdom and attain the "unexcelled-complete-universal-enlightenment" (*anuttara-samyak-sambodhi*, 阿耨多羅三藐三菩提). Hence, they become completely awake and dedicate the rest of their last earthly life helping others become enlightened.

Undoubtedly buddhas are more capable of helping people than bodhisattvas. We may wonder why they are no longer born on

---

4   See for instance, Steiner, *The Influences of Lucifer and Ahriman*.

5   In his book *Theosophy*, p. 121, Steiner uses a simile of many coinciding circles, each retaining its own hue to illustrate this union of the individual spirit with the "All-Spirit."

Chapter 4

Earth like the bodhisattvas. Let us tentatively consider a metaphorical explanation and then study a more profound anthroposophical clarification.

Figuratively speaking, every sentient being on Earth is like an ice patch out in the sea of Universal Consciousness. Now, a bodhisattva unselfishly benefits others. Each time a bodhisattva sacrifices for the sake of others, the ice patch naturally diminishes a little. In other words, during each life of compassionate deeds, the ice patch melts and shrinks somewhat. Therefore, many compassionate lives later, the ice patch will have melted entirely in the Sea of Universal Consciousness. At the moment the ice patch completely disappears, the bodhisattva becomes a buddha. (Please remember that each buddha retains a unique personality as noted earlier.) Thus buddhas, who are one with Universal Consciousness, have no more "ice" to be born on Earth.

Buddhist teachings mention that there were many buddhas in different regions, and some of them are called Pratyeka-Buddhas (*Pì-zhī Fó* 辟支佛).[6] Anthroposophy teaches that, in Western occultism, a buddha is referred to as a "Sun Hero." This name signifies a person, whose spiritual life had found a path as sure as that of the Sun in the heavens and whose soul was in complete harmony with the cosmos. Let us investigate how the clairvoyant Western ancients perceived the inner experience of a Sun Hero:

> How did the ancients conceive of the soul of a Sun Hero who had reached this inner harmony? They believed that he was no longer inhabited solely by an individual human soul; something of the cosmic soul, that permeates the entire universe, had arisen within him. This cosmic Soul was known in Greece as *Chrestos*, in the sublime wisdom of the East as *Budhi*. Those who no longer feel themselves only as bearers of an individual soul, but experience something

---

6 Some Buddhist traditions consider that a Pratyeka-Buddha is not exactly a buddha, but rather a holy *arhat,* or perfected and worthy person.

of the universal Soul, create within themselves an image of the union of the Sun Soul with the human body, attaining a stage in the evolution of humankind which is of the very greatest significance.[7]

Whereas we consider the metaphor of an ice patch entirely melted to allude to the buddha becoming one with Universal Consciousness, Steiner relates an authentic spiritual experience. According to Steiner, there were Sun Heroes among all the peoples just as Buddhist teachings mention there were many buddhas in different regions. In antiquity, the Sun Soul was called by different names. The ancient Persians called him Ahura Mazda, and the seven Indian rishis called him Vishva Karman.[8] Furthermore, the Sun Soul was the "I" of the Christ (*Chrestos*), who was to come to live in a human body on Earth to facilitate the development of the human "I" (or soul).

Buddhas are honored with the title Tathagata, meaning that they are the "one who has thus gone" (*Rú-qù* 如去), or that they are the "one who has thus come" (*Rú-lái* 如來). From the teachings of Anthroposophy, we see that the two seemingly opposite meanings of this title aptly commemorate the same significant event that buddhas have "thus gone" into the Sun Soul and hence are at one with the "thus come" Sun Soul.

Anthroposophy teaches that a human being consists of four members: a physical body, an etheric body, an astral body, and an "I"-being. Human beings developed and are still developing the three bodies together with the "I" (see the appendix for more details). The Christ was waiting for an individual whose "I" could vacate the three bodies and allow His "I" (the Sun Soul) to enter and stay in those vacated bodies. Furthermore, when accommodating the Sun Soul, the three bodies of that individual should be

---

7   Steiner, *The Festivals and Their Meaning*, p. 24.
8   See for instance, Steiner, *According to Matthew*, p. 224.

strong enough to withstand the immense power of the Sun Soul. At last, the saintly man Jesus of Nazareth had developed all the necessary qualities. Thus the Sun Soul entered the three bodies of Jesus of Nazareth during his baptism at the Jordan River and stayed in his bodies for three years.[9]

After the Mystery of Golgotha (the death of Jesus Christ with his blood flowing down on Earth), the Sun Soul permeated the whole Earth and will continue to stay with humanity until the end of the age. Steiner illumines this mystery from many different perspectives in numerous lectures. According to his teachings, this image of death on the Cross is but an external event, and that the life of Christ in the etheric body was the same after as before His death. Christ's death is a demonstration that death in reality is giver of life. Also, the flowing of the blood on Golgotha gave impetus for the gradual disappearance of egoism from the human race. The Christ light that suffused the Earth by degrees will become the seed of a new sun in the universe.[10]

Buddhas in the Three Times

Buddhism teaches that there have been innumerable buddhas before and that there will be innumerable buddhas after. However, Chinese Buddhist tradition tends to honor three particular buddhas in the Three Times: Dīpankara Buddha (*Rándēng Fó* 燃燈佛) as the buddha in the past eon, Gautama Buddha (also known as Buddha Shakyamuni or simply the Buddha) as the buddha in the present eon, and Maitreya Buddha (*Mílè Fó* 彌勒佛) as the buddha in the future eon. Buddhist literature indicates that the earlier buddha predicts who will become the next buddha with a name. For instance, in one of Gautama's previous life, Dīpankara

---

9   See also a later section, "Buddhism and Anthroposophy," in this chapter.
10 See for instance Steiner, *The Gospel of St. John and Its Relation to the Other Gospels,* lect. 13.

Buddha told him that "You, in the ages of the future, would become a buddha called Shakyamuni" (汝於來世，當得作佛，號釋迦牟尼).[11]

Gautama Buddha's journey to buddhahood was long and arduous. He once mentioned that he "remembered during his five hundred previous lives, how he had practiced like an immortal called upon to endure abuse" (又念過去於五百世作忍辱仙人).[12] Gautama told many stories of his previous lives. Let us study one such life story that exemplifies how he had endured abuse like an immortal.

> Eons ago, in a previous life, Gautama was a very poor youth. One day a friend told him that Buddha Shakyamuni Tathagata—this story also discloses why Gautama would also become a buddha by that name—was going to deliver the sermon of *The Mahaparinirvana Sutra*. Gautama wanted to attend the sermon and make an offering to that buddha.
>
> Possessing nothing of value, he went to the market to sell himself for money. Unfortunately no one was interested in buying him. Then, on his way home, he met a man and he causally asked if that man would buy him.
>
> The man replied, "No one can endure the work in my household. If you can, I will buy you."
>
> Gautama inquired what kind of work that no one could endure. The man replied, "I have a bad disease which can only be cured by taking three ounces of human flesh everyday. If you can supply me with three ounces of human flesh daily, I will give you five pieces of gold coins."
>
> Gautama gladly said, "Give me the money and wait seven days for me. After I complete my errand, I will come to work for you." The man said he might wait one day but not seven days. Gautama agreed, took the money, and immediately went to that buddha's place.

---

11   *The Diamond Sutra,* chapter 17.
12   Ibid., chapter 14.

Chapter 4

He prostrated himself to Buddha Shakyamuni Tathagata, offered what he had, and listened attentively to the discourse. However, he could remember nothing except a hymn:

The Tathagata enters nirvana	如來證涅槃
And eternally cuts off samsara.	永斷於生死
If you listen whole-heartedly,	若有至心聽
You'll gain endless bliss constantly.	常得無量樂

Afterward, Gautama went back to the sick man to whom he daily gave three ounces of his own flesh. A month later, the man's disease was cured. Gautama indicated that in cutting his flesh he neither felt pain nor suffered any after ill effect. He considered the nirvana hymn had sustained him all those time. He was deeply grateful for that Buddha Shakyamuni Tathagata. He vowed in a future life to become a buddha by that name and to teach people this sutra.[13]

Eons later (c. 563 BCE), Gautama was born as Prince Siddhartha Gautama in the Shakya clan—incidentally Shakyamuni means the sage of Shakya. When he was a newborn, a hermit came to the palace to see him and predicted that if he became a king he would be a great ruler uniting all India, or if he became a monk he would be a buddha saving numerous sentient beings. Avoiding any motivation for Siddhartha to become a monk, his father raised him inside the confines of the palace and shielded him from any experience of human misery.

At age twenty-nine, he decided to travel outside the palace without his father's knowledge. When he was outside, he saw a sick person, an old person, and a corpse. He felt great sorrow for people's miseries. He immediately forsook the court to seek relief of human suffering. Then at age thirty-five, he became fully

---

13 *The Mahaparinirvana Sutra*, ch. 22 (paraphrased); www.cbeta.org/result/normal/T12/0374_022.htm.

enlightened under the bodhi tree.¹⁴ Thereafter, until his death at about the age of eighty, he unceasingly expounded the dharma to enlighten sentient beings.

In one of his sermons, Gautama Buddha predicted,

> In the distant future,...there will arise in the world a buddha named Maitreya Tathagata,...even as I am now a Tathagata. (未來久遠,...當有佛，名彌勒如來...猶如我今已成如來.)¹⁵

Although several Buddhist scriptures mention Maitreya as the next buddha, the exact time of his buddhahood is not quite clear. On the Internet, there are speculations galore that Maitreya had appeared as a buddha or was none other than the Christ. However, Rudolf Steiner teaches that Maitreya will appear as the next buddha five thousand years after Gautama Buddha. He puts forth a profound discourse on how Maitreya prepares for his buddhahood that merits our earnest perusal.

Buddhism and Anthroposophy

Anthroposophy offers insightful perspectives on the relationship between Buddhism and esoteric Christianity. We shall first recount a story that concerns Gautama Buddha and the young Jesus, and then study more closely the connection between Maitreya and Jesus Christ.

Rudolf Steiner delivered many lectures on Gautama Buddha's past and continuing contributions to humankind. We ask above why buddhas who are more capable of helping people are no longer born

---

14 In *Background to the Gospel of St. Mark,* lect. 5, Steiner notes that being "under the bodhi tree" is a symbolic expression for a certain enhancement of consciousness. The mystic life opens a path by which the human "I" can enter its own Being, or deeper nature. What Gautama Buddha experienced in this outstanding descent is described as "The Temptation of Buddha" in Buddhist writings.

15 *Majjhima Nikaya* (*Zhōng-ā-hán Jīng* 中阿含經), chapter 13; www.cbeta.org/result/normal/T01/0026_013.htm.

Chapter 4

on Earth. It turns out that buddhas do not need to be reincarnated to benefit humanity as shown in the following story.

In one of Rudolf Steiner's lecture cycles, *According to Luke*, he indicates that one can confirm from the akashic record (the memory of the cosmos) that Gautama Buddha continues to influence the Earth through his astral body, his Nirmanakaya (*Yīnghuà-shēn* 應化身). In lectures 2 and 3, Steiner relates that Buddha's Nirmanakaya appeared in the form of a host of angels to the shepherds during the nativity of Jesus,[16] and continued to shine on the child Jesus afterward. Then a significant event occurred to the Nirmanakaya when Jesus was twelve, at the start of his puberty.

Recall that Anthroposophy teaches that a human being consists of four members: a physical body, an etheric body, an astral body, and an "I"-being. They begin at different times, generally seven years apart.

> In physical birth, an individual sheds the physical mother's covering, as it were. The mother's etheric covering, which surrounds the child until the second dentition just as her physical body surrounds the infant until physical birth, is discarded in the seventh year of life. At puberty, which presently occurs in the year of fourteenth or fifteenth year of life, the astral covering is discarded.... In Palestine... puberty typically began earlier—during the twelfth year of life.[17]

Steiner remarks that when the boy Jesus was twelve, the protective astral covering was discarded and was united with the Nirmanakaya of the Buddha. This union made it possible for the Buddha's expression of his wisdom to reappear in the childlike simplicity of the boy Jesus, just as Buddha's ancient Indian teachings

---

16 Some shepherds were out in the field at night, when an angel proclaimed to them the birth of a savior. Suddenly there was with the angel a multitude of the heavenly host praising God and saying, "Glory to God in highest heaven, and peace on Earth to those with whom God is pleased" (see Luke, 2:8–14).

17 Steiner, *According to Luke*, pp. 77–78.

were made suitable for the people of that time. Jesus demonstrated the union by how he spoke at his visit to the temple, astonishing those around him by his wisdom.[18]

In another lecture course, *Esoteric Christianity and the Mission of Christian Rosenkreutz*, Steiner again touches on various aspects of Buddhism. He focuses on the future Maitreya Buddha in two of these lectures, which we now examine more fully. While summarizing his narrative on Maitreya we also supplement with anthroposophic background materials for clarity. Please note that to enhance easy reading, we omit mentioning Steiner's name.

Maitreya, right after ascending to the rank of a bodhisattva during the time of Gautama Buddha, "has since then, been incarnated once in nearly every century" to bring humanity forward.[19] In each incarnation, he "develops in the highest degree what we may describe as devotion, serenity in the presence of destiny, attentiveness to all occurrences in one's surroundings, devotion to all living beings, and insight."[20] For his ascent from the rank of a bodhisattva to that of a buddha, about five thousand years—or equivalently about fifty-two earthly lives corresponding to the fifty-two steps—are needed. He is utterly devoted to the preparation of his future mission so that when he becomes the buddha, he will be able to "impart heart forces and moral impulses to human souls through the word itself."[21] "He will be the one whom the sufficiently clairvoyant ancients foresaw: the Maitreya Buddha, a Bringer of Good."[22]

---

18 At the age of twelve, Jesus and his parents went to Jerusalem for the feast of Passover. When the feast was over, Jesus stayed behind without his parents' knowledge. Three days later, his parents found him in the temple sitting among the teachers, who were listening to him and asking him questions. All who heard him were amazed at his understanding and his answers (Luke, 2:41–50).
19 Steiner, *Esoteric Christianity*, pp. 125–126.
20 Ibid., p. 126.
21 Ibid.
22 Ibid., p. 110.

Chapter 4

Approximately one hundred years before Jesus Christ, Maitreya lived as an Essene teacher named Jeshu ben Pandira. In that life, Maitreya was stoned to death and was then hanged upon the beam of a cross as a herald of the Christ in the physical body. Afterward, in every subsequent incarnation, Maitreya patterns his life on that of Jesus Christ.

According to esoteric Christianity, the greatest transformation of the life of Jesus of Nazareth happened at his thirtieth year during his baptism at the Jordan River. "What occurred there was that the 'I' of Jesus, in the thirtieth year of his life, abandoned the flesh, and another 'I'—the 'I' of the Christ, the Leader of the Sun Beings—entered."[23]

In another lecture cycle, Steiner explains more fully that the "I" of Jesus left his three bodies moments before going to the Jordan River. Then during his baptism, the "I" of the Christ entered these bodies. Henceforth, the Christ Spirit united more and more closely with the bodies of Jesus of Nazareth and only united completely three years later, just before the Mystery of Golgotha.[24]

Let us return to the lectures in *Esoteric Christianity and the Mission of Christian Rosenkreutz* and continue to study how Maitreya patterns his life on that of Jesus Christ.

> It will always be noted that, in the period between his thirtieth and thirty-third years, a mighty revolution occurs in his life. There will then be an interchange of souls, though not in so mighty a manner as in the case of Christ. The "I," which has until then given life to the body, passes out at that time, and the bodhisattva becomes, in a fundamental sense, altogether a different person from what he has been hitherto, even though the "I," does not cease and is not replaced by another, as was true of the Christ.[25]

---

23 Ibid., p. 126 (tr. rev.). In the citation here and hereafter, "the flesh" or "the body" refers to the three bodies.

24 Steiner, *The Fifth Gospel*, pp. 225–227 (tr. rev.).

25 Ibid., p. 127 (tr. rev.).

In each of Maitreya's subsequent incarnations after Jesus Christ, from the age of thirty to the age of thirty-three, his "I" will partly recede from his three bodies and let the "I" of another individuality such as Moses, Abraham, or Elijah enter and permeate them. When this process stops, he lives as an individual with a transformed personality.

> And when he appears after 3,000 years,[26] and has been elevated to the rank of Maitreya Buddha, his "I" will remain in him but will be permeated inwardly by still another individuality. And this will occur precisely in his thirty-third year, in the year in which, in the case of Christ, the Mystery of Golgotha occurred. And then will he come forth as the Teacher of the Good, as a great Teacher who will prepare the true teaching of Christ and the true wisdom of Christ in a manner entirely different from what is possible today."[27]

From this study, we learn that in about 2,500 years from now (year 2014, see note 26), Maitreya will be a great teacher of the Christ impulse. Steiner stresses that the future Maitreya Buddha will appear in his thirty-third year without being proclaimed by anyone. "It would be sheer occult dilettantism to assert that he would be recognized in his early years. He would reveal himself through his own power without being proclaimed by others."[28]

Rudolf Steiner indicates that in the future, people will be able to see that inner goodness works differently on the environment from evil and that Maitreya Buddha is the person who possesses this science in the highest degree. In lecture 3 of yet another course entitled, *The Reappearance of Christ in the Etheric*, Steiner reiterates,

---

26 The number 3,000 is an approximation. Counting 5,000 years from the time when Gautama became the Buddha, we reckon that in 1911, when Steiner gave these two lectures, the number of years remaining were about 2,600.

27 Ibid., pp. 127–128. As related previously, he would be able to "impart heart forces and moral impulses to human souls through the word itself."

28 Ibid., p. 42.

"*Maitreya Buddha* means the 'Buddha of right-mindedness.' He is the one who will make human beings aware of the significance of right thinking."

Thus, Anthroposophy discloses that the religious streams of Buddhism and esoteric Christianity are subtly entwined. On the one hand, the Gospel of Luke relates a new form of Buddhism rejuvenated by the youthful Jesus. On the other hand, the future Maitreya Buddha will inspire people to follow the teachings of Christ to think rightly and be inwardly good, helping civilization evolve fruitfully toward the future.

Chapter 5

故知般若波羅蜜多，是大神咒，是大明咒，是無上咒，是無等等咒，能除一切苦，真實不虛，故說般若波羅蜜多咒。即說咒曰，

揭諦，揭諦，波羅揭諦，波羅僧揭諦，菩提薩婆訶。

> Therefore one should know that the perfection of wisdom is the great spiritual mantra, the mantra of great understanding, the supreme mantra, and the mantra equal to the unequalled. It can allay all suffering and is the truth not falsehood. By the prajnaparamita has this mantra been extolled and it says:
>
> *Gate, gate, paragate, parasamgate, bodhi svaha!*

Mantras

The Heart Sutra summarizes Buddhism succinctly. It briefly mentions Buddha's early teachings and concisely covers the main points of Mahayana Buddhism. This last passage uses a mantra to further capture the essence of the practice of the perfection of wisdom. We shall acquaint ourselves with two other Buddhist mantras to enhance our appreciation of this one.

In chapter 1, we learned that Avalokitesvara knows all mantras, and we then explored the significance of the chant "Homage to Bodhisattva Avalokitesvara" (*Nā-mó Guān-shì-yīn pú-sà* 南無觀世音菩薩). Now, let us consider a well-known six-syllable mantra: *om mani padme hum* 唵嘛呢叭咪吽.[1] In *The Karandavyuha Sutra* (*Fó Shuì Dà-chéng Zhuāng-yán Bǎo Wáng Jīng* 佛說大乘莊嚴寶王經), chapter 4,

---

1   For a scholarly account on the merits and historical origin of this mantra, see Studholme, *The Origins of Om Manipadme Hum: A Study of the Karandavyuha Sutra*.

Gautama Buddha relates a meandering story on how he got to hear this mantra revealed by Bodhisattva Avalokitesvara.

The syllables *om* and *hum* are sacred interjections, *mani* means jewel and *padme* means lotus. *Om* is the creative world word.[2] The sound *om*, actually consists of three sounds A-U-M. In Hinduism, these three sounds stand for both the process and the energy of the Universe. While the beginning of the Universe's process is A, the duration U, and the dissolution M, its energy is characterized by form, which is A, formless U, and neither form nor formless M.[3] However, in Buddhism, A-U-M is used to represent the diamond body, speech, and mind of enlightened beings.

The six-syllable mantra, which symbolizes Avalokitesvara holding the precious lotus, is likened to a hook with which he can liberate sentient beings.[4] According to Tibetan Buddhist teachings, this mantra contains profound tantric meanings and bestows great divine virtues. People who resolutely recite it will gain relief from suffering, innumerable merits, and enlightenment. Moreover, those who just look at the script or hear the chant of this mantra may also obtain significant blessings. Therefore this mantra is deeply ingrained in the livelihood of Tibetan Buddhists. The photos on page 69 show its ubiquitous presence and hence influence in their society.

Another mantra: "Homage to Buddha Amitabha" (*Nā-mó Ē-mí-tuó-fó* 南無阿彌陀佛), is immensely popular in the Pure Land Buddhist tradition. The name Amitabha, which means unlimited light, can in effect be applied to all buddhas. Therefore reciting this mantra is in a sense paying homage to all buddhas. According to the Pure Land teachings, people who diligently recite Buddha Amitabha will after death be born in his Pure Land, the Western World of

---

2   Some ancient occultists such as the old Pythagoreans spoke of the consciousness of the creative world word as hearing the music of the spheres (see, for instance, Steiner, *Mystery of the Universe,* lect. 16).

3   See, for instance, www.en.wikipedia.org/wiki/Om.

4   See Sonam, *The Heart Sutra*, p. 77.

Chapter 5

Top: "Om mani padme hum" in Tibetan Script
near the Potala Palace in Lhasa, Tibet
(www.en.wikipedia.org/wiki/File:Om_Mani_Padme_Hum.jpg);

Bottom: "Om mani padme hum" carved in stones
in Zangskar, Ladakh, India
(www.en.wikipedia.org/wiki/File:Mune_wall_col.jpg)

Eternal Bliss. When they are born there, Buddha Amitabha will directly teach them to attain enlightenment.

Someone once asked the Sixth Patriarch of Zen Huìnéng 惠能 to comment on this practice of reciting Buddha Amitabha to be born in the Western Pure Land. He responded,

> When your mind is free from evil, the West is not far from here; but when you keep an evil heart, reciting Buddha [Amitabha] can hardly help you be born there. (使君心地，但無不善，西方去此不遙；若懷不善之心，念佛往生難到。)[5]

According to Huìnéng, the best way to realize our inborn buddha nature is to cultivate a good heart. He once averred,

> We inherently have buddha nature, the wisdom of prajna. It is only because of the delusion of our mind that we cannot realize it ourselves. Hence, we need fully enlightened masters to guide us to realize our own nature. (菩提般若之智，世人本自有之，只緣心迷，不能自悟，須假大善知識，示導見性。)[6]

Remember those Zen students who are unaware that they are holding a lamp and need their teacher to point out the truth. Huìnéng's own enlightenment story is an apt case in point:

> In his youth, Huìnéng was a poor illiterate firewood seller living with his widowed mother in a southern province of China. One day, after delivering firewood, he heard a traveller recite *The Diamond Sutra*, and at once, his mind became clear. He asked the traveller where he got this teaching. The traveller replied that he learned it in the county of Huáng-méi 黃梅 (in a northern province), from the Fifth Patriarch of Zen Hóngrěn 弘忍, who taught reciting *The Diamond Sutra* as a way to realize buddha nature. Huìnéng wanted to visit Huáng-méi to pay homage to this Fifth Patriarch. A kind

---

5   *The Platform Sutra of the Sixth Patriarch*, chapter 3.
6   Ibid., chapter 2.

customer gave him money so that he could arrange care for his widowed mother and make the trip.

In about a month, Huìnéng reached Huáng-méi and had an audience with the Fifth Patriarch, who asked him why he came. Huìnéng expressed his desire to realize buddha nature. Recognizing Huìnéng's clear mind, the Fifth Patriarch was afraid that deluded people might harm him and therefore assigned him to work in the kitchen temporarily.

After about eight months, one day the Fifth Patriarch asked monks in his monastery to write a poem about meditation so that he could determine his successor. At first, only the head monk Shénxiù 神秀 posted such a poem in the hallway in front of the Fifth Patriarch's residence. Later, in the kitchen, Huìnéng heard someone recite Shénxiù's poem. He asked that person to take him to pay respects to this poem. At the site, a visitor read out this poem for him. After hearing it read out, he had a poem composed and requested that the visitor write down his poem next to Shénxiù's.[7]

The poems clearly indicated that Huìnéng understood the empty nature of bodhi but Shénxiù did not. Thus the Fifth Patriarch promoted Huìnéng to be the Sixth Patriarch without fanfare, privately taught him *The Diamond Sutra*, but advised him to temporary hide to avoid unnecessary persecutions by deluded people. Huìnéng kept himself hidden among bands of hunters for about fifteen years before going public with his illuminative teachings.[8]

The Prajnaparamita Mantra

Here, in this last passage of *The Heart Sutra*, Bodhisattva Avalokita exhorts all those who seek enlightenment to regard the prajnaparamita (the perfection of wisdom) as the great spiritual mantra, the mantra of great understanding, the supreme mantra, and the mantra equal to the unequalled.

---

7 See chapter 3, page 45.
8 *The Platform Sutra of the Sixth Patriarch,* chapter 1 (paraphrased).

As the great spiritual mantra, the prajnaparamita eliminates obstacles from the mind, entailing practitioners to perceive that form and emptiness are basically not different. As the mantra of great understanding, the prajnaparamita dispels inverted delusions, illuminating practitioners to conceive that all dharmas are a semblance of emptiness. As the supreme mantra, the prajnaparamita shows the path to the beyond, guiding practitioners to eventually enter nirvana. As the mantra is equal to the unequalled, the prajnaparamita bestows complete awakening, ushering practitioners to attain the unexcelled-complete-universal-enlightenment.

Recall Steiner's comment on the enlightenment experience of buddhas: "Those who no longer feel themselves only as bearers of an individual soul, but experience something of the universal Soul, create within themselves an image of the union of the Sun Soul with the human body, attaining a stage in the evolution of humankind which is of the very greatest significance" (see chapter 4, pp. 55–56). Indeed, the Dalai Lama remarks that "the Buddha's enlightened state is unequalled and through the deepest realization of this mantra, one attains a state equal to that state."[9] Arriving at that state, one recognizes that Universal Consciousness is true and not false, and experiences no suffering but "eternity, joy, the Self, and purity."

This is how the prajnaparamita mantra is recited:

Gate, gate, paragate, parasamgate, bodhi svaha!

Loosely it means, "Gone, gone, gone beyond, gone completely beyond. Awakened! All hail!" This mantra is a summary of the course of the perfection of wisdom. The four "gone" (*gate* 揭諦) refers to the three phases of the course. The first and the second *gone* deal with the two preparatory phases of the course, while the

---

9   The Dalai Lama, *Essence of the Heart Sutra: The Dalai Lama's Heart of Wisdom Teachings*, p. 130.

third and the fourth *gone* focus on the beyond phase.[10] Let us review these three phases using the three interpretations of the name *Shè-lì-zi* 舍利子.

First: "form is no different from emptiness, and emptiness is no different from form. Whatever is form is emptiness and whatever is emptiness is form." Practitioners as represented by Sariputra perceive the empty nature of matters. They are *gone* from dwelling on material profits (*lì-yì* 利益).

Second: Bodhisattva Avalokita repeatedly uses negatives to reinforce the idea that all dharmas are a semblance of emptiness. The story of Jùzhī 俱胝 cutting off his boy attendant's finger symbolizes the letting go of all dharmas. Practitioners as represented by Sariputra are *gone* from grasping expedient means (*biàn-lì* 便利).

Third: "Without aiming for attainment, and only relying on the perfection of wisdom, bodhisattvas find no obstacles in the mind. With no obstacles, they have no fear. They depart afar from inverted delusions, and eventually enter nirvana." During the third phase, practitioners have *gone beyond* from accumulating their own benefits (*fú-lì* 福利). They compassionately perfect themselves for the benefit of others. They continue this practice until they have *gone completely beyond* realizing the unexcelled-complete-universal-enlightenment. When awakening to such a "greatly free and comfortable" (*dà-zì-zài* 大自在) state, they are automatically filled with "great mercy" (*dà cí-bēi* 大慈悲). Their joy is to benefit all sentient beings selflessly.

Great Blessings

In this short commentary, we analyze *The Heart Sutra* with simple metaphors, exceptional stories, illuminative Buddhist scriptures, applicable Taoist writings, and relevant teachings of Anthroposophy.

---

10 Pertaining to the four members of a human being as taught in Anthroposophy, we may also regard the four *gone* as the four steps in cleansing and purifying the physical body, the etheric body, the astral body, and the "I"-being.

We learn that the foundation of our existence is Intelligence, which is the unmanifest light, the consciousness without knowledge of an object, and the unspoken word. *The Heart Sutra* begins with Bodhisattva Avalokitesvara observing his foundation of existence in light. Most of the exposition in *The Heart Sutra* is about the unmanifest light and the consciousness without knowledge of an object. However, at the end, bodhisattva Avalokitesvara announces the mystical power of the "word" with a mantra completing the circle of his teachings.

We rejoice that we may realize buddha nature by just chanting an extremely brief and concise prajnaparamita mantra without having to recite a long scripture such as *The Diamond Sutra* or even this much shorter *Heart Sutra*. Meditating on the mantra and following its teachings can help us miraculously convert all pain and suffering into mercy and compassion, leading us to experience "eternity, joy, the Self, and purity." O, what great blessings Bodhisattva Avalokitesvara bestows.

Appendix: A Brief Introduction to Anthroposophy

Anthroposophy is a study of the spiritual world propagated by the Austrian spiritual teacher Rudolf Steiner. He referred to his study as a *Spiritual Science*, because he investigated the spiritual world with the same rigorous principles that natural scientists use to investigate the physical world. He wrote extensively and presented more than six thousand lectures to explain how human evolution is related to the spiritual world.

Steiner indicated that anyone who has fully developed the spiritual organs will be able to read the akashic record (the memory of the cosmos) in the spiritual world and learn how human beings and the cosmos are interrelated and evolve in parallel. He developed many meditative exercises to help students awaken their dormant spiritual organs. Nonetheless, he frequently remarked that once spiritual facts have been investigated they can be understood by healthy human reason and ordinary experience. Therefore, it is not necessary to develop spiritual organs to comprehend Anthroposophy.

1. *The Four Members of the Human Being*

Steiner teaches that each human being consists of four members, or principles: a physical body, an etheric body, an astral body, and an "I"-being. Only the physical body is visible, but the other three members are invisible. Nevertheless, comparing the similarities and differences of the four kingdoms of humans, animals, plants, and minerals can readily illustrate the functions of these four principles.

First, human beings, animals, and plants have physical bodies, which are composed of minerals. Second, these physical bodies are not merely minerals since they are alive with an etheric (life) principle, which minerals lack. Third, humans and animals are "higher" than plants because they have an astral body, which is the seat of feelings, emotions, and perceptions that plants do not have. Fourth, humans are the highest because they have an "I," or self-awareness, which animals generally lack. The "I" enables humans to use the brain to reason and facilitate remembrance of past events. The life experiences of human beings are reflected in the astral body. These images are imparted later to the etheric body, which imprints them again into the physical body and the "I" accesses those impressions as memory.

These four interconnecting members or principles intricately influence and work for one another. For example, the organs of the physical body work for all four members. To a certain extent, we can say that the mechanical organs work for the physical body itself, the glandular organs for the etheric body, the nerve organs for the astral body, and the circulatory blood system for the "I."

Basically, the etheric body and physical body are closely knitted as a lower unit. Men have a masculine physical body but a feminine etheric body; conversely, women have a feminine physical body but a masculine etheric body. In this sense, all human beings are both male and female. The Swiss psychologist Carl Jung (1875–1961) intuited the dual aspect of human existence and stated that a man's inner personality is female, the anima, and that a woman's is male, the animus.

Complementing the lower unit, the "I" and the astral body are entwined as a higher unit. When people sleep, the higher unit leaves the lower unit and returns when they wake up. (Strictly speaking, the higher unit only leaves the head portion of the lower unit.) Indeed, after a day's work of feeling, thinking, and willing in the etheric and physical bodies, the "I" and the astral body become exhausted and need to replenish their forces in the spiritual world. During their absence, a substitute "I" and astral being of divine spirituality maintain their systems of the nerves and circulation. Upon waking, the higher members return with renewed vigor. However, since the etheric body is not with the two higher members during sleep, it receives no impressions from the astral body of their activities. Hence, most people (those who are not clairvoyant) have no memory of what happens during sleep.

In ancient times, initiates guided by a teacher were induced to a special state of sleep, also referred to as the temple sleep, upon which the etheric body could be raised out of the physical body to accompany the two higher members. After about three and a half days, the neophytes were awakened by their teacher and would gradually recall their experiences in the spiritual world. Steiner explains that in our era, the etheric body is united too closely with the physical body as a lower unit, and such a method is no longer suitable. He says since the Christ event, human beings can gain spiritual knowledge by developing their spiritual organs, thus eliminating the need to draw out the etheric body.

Throughout life, the four members commingle during waking hours. However, when asleep the "I" and the astral body leave the etheric and physical bodies (more precisely leave the head portion of these bodies) and return when awake. At death, the "I" and the astral body, together with the etheric body, discard the physical body and never return to it. After death, the physical body without the life principle slowly decays to the elements, while the etheric body reveals the record of the recently lived life like a great "tableau." The "I" reviews this record in reverse order for about three days. Then the etheric body dissolves into the cosmic forces and the "I" keeps its essence. The "I" then purifies the astral body for a period that lasts about one-third of the lived years. For instance, those who die at the age of ninety will spend about thirty years cleansing their astral body. Afterward, the astral body also dissolves into the cosmos and the "I" retains its essence as well. Then the "I" continues to develop in the spiritual realm until a new birth.

Moreover, only humans have their three higher members permeating the physical body—two repeatedly leave during sleep but return when awake while all three leave at death without returning. However, the "I" of animals does not occupy the animal bodies at all but simply stays in the spiritual realm; the "I" and the astral body of plants do so similarly, whereas the "I," the astral body, and the etheric body of minerals always remain in the spiritual world.[1]

2. Development of Consciousness

According to Anthroposophy, human beings first had a very dim consciousness, much like that of the minerals. It has taken them eons to develop from this dim consciousness to a self-aware consciousness. Human consciousness evolved long ago and will continue to evolve far into the future. In esoteric terms, the evolution of consciousness is divided into seven "planetary" phases (or Days), named Saturn, Sun, Moon, Earth, Jupiter, Venus, and Vulcan. Please note that these esoteric terms refer to the phases of the planet Earth, not the heavenly bodies they represent today.

The days of a week reflect this esoteric knowledge, highlighting humanity's past, present, and future evolution. Saturday is named for Saturn's Day; Sunday for Sun's Day; Monday for Moon's Day; Tuesday for Mars's Day (the first half of the Earth phase before the Christ event of Golgotha); Wednesday for Mercury's Day (the second half since Christ); Thursday for Thor's (or Jupiter's) Day; and Friday for Venus's Day. Vulcan is not included in the weekdays.

During the Saturn phase (also referred to as old Saturn) of cosmic evolution, the spiritual hierarchies—whose names and special functions during the Earth phase are outlined in section 4—endowed human beings with a physical body. It consisted of only warmth

---

[1] For more on this profound topic of the four members, please consult anthroposophic literature.

Appendix: A Brief Introduction to Anthroposophy

and was quite unlike the solid physical body people now have. Laws of the physical body were established, and they developed a deep-trance consciousness. The present minerals are entities with such a deep-trance consciousness as on old Saturn. Old Saturn ended with a long period of rest.[2]

The Sun phase (old Sun) started after a long rest from old Saturn. It first recapitulated the developments of old Saturn. Afterward the hierarchies added an etheric body to the evolving physical body. Intelligence imbued the etheric body, and human beings developed a consciousness like dreamless sleep. Plants of today are entities with dreamless sleep consciousness, such as on old Sun. Old Sun also ended with a long period of rest.

The Moon phase (old Moon) started after old Sun and recapitulated the earlier developments of old Saturn and old Sun. Then an astral body was added to the evolving etheric body and physical body. Human beings developed a consciousness like dream-filled sleep with feelings and emotions. Animals of today are those with dream-filled sleep consciousness, such as on old Moon. Again, old Moon ended with a long period of rest.

This pattern of recapitulation and rest are also followed by all subsequent planetary phases. During the present Earth phase, an "I"-being has been added, and human beings have been developing and shall continue to develop a waking consciousness. We shall explore this phase more fully in section 3.

In future planetary evolutions, the three bodies will become spiritualized. In the Jupiter phase, the astral body will become "spirit self" (also called *manas*), and human beings will attain an *Imagination* (psychic) consciousness. In the Venus phase, the etheric body will become "life spirit" (*buddhi*), and people will attain an *Inspiration*

---

2 Please note that a "rest period" always takes place between succeeding planetary phases. Moreover, the subsequent phase always recapitulates the earlier developments before starting any new activity.

(super-psychic) consciousness. In the Vulcan phase, the physical body will become "spirit body" (*atma*), and human beings will attain an *Intuition* (spiritual) consciousness. These future stages of consciousness evolution are still very faraway. For now during the Earth phase, human beings are developing waking consciousness.

The following table[3] shows the consciousness condition with the planetary evolution:

Planetary Evolution	State of Consciousness	Demonstrated today as
old Saturn	deep trance	minerals
old Sun	dreamless sleep	plants
old Moon	dream-filled sleep	animals
Earth	waking/object	human beings
Jupiter	imagination (psychic)	Earth + Moon
Venus	inspiration (super-psychic)	sound
Vulcan	intuition (spiritual)	identification of self with spiritual beings

3. Evolution of the "I"

We can distinguish two parts of the "I." The higher "I" is the "Christ spirit," and the lower "I" is the soul. For most human beings, the Christ spirit is only a seed or embryo during the present Earth phase evolution. It will manifest its full functions in future planetary evolutions. The main task of people during the present Earth phase is to develop the soul, which they customarily refer to as the "I."

---

3   Adapted from Smith, *The Burning Bush*, p. 622.

Appendix: A Brief Introduction to Anthroposophy

As stated, the three bodies (physical, etheric, and astral) were prepared eons ago, during three earlier planetary evolutionary phases. In the initial period of the present Earth phase, human beings (with the help of the spiritual hierarchies) recapitulate the earlier developments of the three bodies and then continue to evolve with the soul as an instrument.

We can separate the soul into three elements according to their functions in the three bodies. The elements, which develop progressively one after another, are: the "sentient soul" in the astral body, the "intellectual soul" (or mind soul) in the etheric body, and the "consciousness soul" in the physical body. As the soul began its development, people gradually lost clairvoyance and the direct guidance from the hierarchies. This was probably the time when "the Great *Tao* recedes," as referred to by Laozi (*The Tao Te Ching*, chapter 18). With this development, humans slowly become freethinking beings.

Briefly, the sentient soul, which is the awareness of sensory experience, developed from around 3000 to 800 BCE. The intellectual soul, related to people's awareness of the experience between their being and thinking, developed from around 800 BCE to 1400 CE. The consciousness soul, bringing awareness of objective reality of the external world in contrast to people's inner self, developed around 1400 and will continue to evolve until about 3600. (We summarize the soul development in the table on page 82.)

Designating the eras for the soul's evolution is simply a convenient way to indicate which particular soul element is actively developing in what time. Indeed, each soul element begins to develop in seed form during the preceding era and matures in the subsequent era. Human beings are now actively developing a consciousness of the outer world and the inner self. This may explain why nowadays people tend to be materialistic and egoistic. They have to know and understand thoroughly the external physical world and the inner spiritual self before they can transcend both and realize the Christ spirit.

Element	sentient soul	intellectual soul	consciousness soul
Active Epoch	3000–800 B.C.E.	800 B.C.E.–C.E. 1400	C.E. 1400–3600
Vessel	astral body	etheric body	physical body
Awareness	sensory	being and thinking	reality of outer world and inner self

4. The Spiritual Hierarchies and the Evolution of Earth

We now focus on the evolution of the planet Earth, which runs parallel (and is interrelated) to the evolution of human consciousness. We only sketch from the Saturn phase to the beginning stages of the present Earth phase. Please keep in mind that this information is gathered through spiritual investigations of the akashic record.

Rudolf Steiner explained that there are nine hierarchies between humankind and the Trinity of Father, Son, and Holy Spirit, and that the manifestation of the Trinity arose through the works (or thoughts) of the spiritual hierarchies. The table on page 83 lists the names of the nine hierarchies Steiner used (with the traditional Roman or Greek Christian names in parentheses). In the column on the right are their manifestations during the present Earth phase.[4]

During the Saturn phase (old Saturn), the Spirits of Will (3) were mainly responsible for the *Earth* then. They poured warmth (fire) ether over the planet. The other hierarchies were also helping and evolving. After their extensive activities, a long period of rest ensued.

The Earth was then awakened to old Sun, its second phase of cosmic evolution, during which phase the Spirits of Wisdom (4) were mainly responsible. Initially, all the hierarchies recapitulated their previous developments. Then, new elements of rarefied light

---

[4] Adapted from Smith, *The Burning Bush*, pp. 556, 600.

Appendix: A Brief Introduction to Anthroposophy

1. Spirits of Love (seraphim)	lightning/fire
2. Spirits of Harmony (cherubim)	clouds/air
3. Spirits of Will (thrones/thronos)	solid matter
4. Spirits of Wisdom (dominions/kyriotetes)	life
5. Spirits of Motion (mights/dynamis)	chemical/sound
6. Spirits of Form (powers/exusiai)	light
7. Spirits of Personality (principality/archai)	fire
8. Spirits of Fire (archangels/archangeloi)	air
9. Sons of Life (angels/angeloi)	water

ether and denser air ether were added to the warmth ether. Again, a long rest ensued after their lengthy work.

Afterward, the third phase, old Moon began. The Spirits of Motion (5) were mainly responsible. New elements of rarefied sound (chemical) ether and denser water (liquid) ether were added.

The Earth phase, which is the fourth stage of cosmic evolution, began after a long rest from old Moon. The Spirits of Form (6) are mainly responsible, with the other hierarchies helping, as shown in the table above. New elements of rarefied life ether and denser earth (solid) ether have been added. Before describing in some detail about the initial periods of the Earth phase, we list on page 84 a table of the ether elements that are active during the four planetary phases, with the newly added ethers in italics.[5]

---

5   The four ethers: earth, water, air, and warmth (fire), listed in the right column of the table, correspond to the four great elements as taught in Buddhism. Since ethers are creations (thoughts) of the hierarchies, they are in essence empty. Cf. chapter 2.

Saturn	Sun	Moon	Earth
			life
		sound	sound
	light	light	light
warmth	warmth	warmth	warmth
	air	air	air
		water	water
			earth

In the beginning of the Earth phase, all the ether elements are in a chaotic mix. As the hierarchies recapitulate the three earlier planetary developments, with their forces cyclically moving in and out through the mixture, the ether elements gradually separate. From this chaotic etheric mixture, first the thrones (3) excrete the water ether, then the cherubim (2) the air ether, and the seraphim (1) the warmth ether. The Spirits of Form (6) bring them into solid forms. While the Spirits of Wisdom (4) pour life ether into the forms, the Spirits of Motion (5) add sound ether into them. The Spirits of Personality (7), which are also called Spirits of Age, are responsible for human history.[6] In addition, the archangels (8) serve as "folk spirits" (the spirits of nations and peoples), while angels (9) act as intermediaries between human beings and the folk spirits.[7]

---

6   See Steiner, *Genesis: Secrets of Creation,* chapter 5.

7   This brief introduction to Anthroposophy is a slightly modified version of appendix 1 in my other book, *Lao Tzu and Anthroposophy.*

Selected Bibliography

Chödrön, Pema. *The Wisdom of No Escape and the Path of Loving-Kindness.* Boston: Shambhala, 1991.

Cleary, Thomas (tr.). *The Sutra of Hui-neng, Grand Master of Zen.* Boston: Shambhala, 1998.

——— (tr.). *Unlocking the Zen Koan: A New Translation of the Zen Classic Wumenguam.* Berkeley, CA: North Atlantic Books, 1997.

Conze, Edward. *Buddhist Meditation.* Dover edition, Mineola, NY: Dover, 2003.

——— (tr.). *Buddhist Wisdom: The Diamond Sutra and The Heart Sutra.* New York: Random House, 2001.

Dalai Lama, The. *Dzogchen: The Heart Essence of The Great Perfection.* Ithaca, NY: Snow Lion Publications, 2000.

———. *Essence of the Heart Sutra: The Dalai Lama's Heart of Wisdom Teachings.* Somerville, MA: Wisdom Publications, 2005.

Dong Chu Old Monk 東初老和尚. *Bō-rě Xīn Jīng Sī Xiǎng Shǐ* 般若心經思想史. Taiwan: 法鼓, 1997.

Faha 法海 (ed.). *The Platform Sutra of the Sixth Patriarch* 六祖大師法寶壇經.

Hayward, J. W., and F. J. Varela. *Gentle Bridges: Conversations with the Dalai Lama on the Sciences of Mind.* Boston: Shambhala Publications, 2014.

M. (Mahendrannath Gupta), *The Gospel of Sri Ramakrishna* (tr. Swami Nikhilananda). New York: Ramakrishna-Vivekananda Center, 1942.

Nán, Huáijǐn 南懷瑾. *Guānyīn Púsà Yǔ Guānyīn Fǎmén* 觀音菩薩與觀音法門. Taipei, Taiwan: 老古文化事業公司, 1985.

———. *Selected Work of Nán Huáijǐn* (vol. 8). *Jīn-gāng Jīng Shuō Shénme* 金剛經說甚麼. Shanghai: Fudan Univ. Press, 2003.

———. *Selected Work of Nán Huáijǐn* (vol. 8). *Léngyán Dàyì Jīn Shì* 楞嚴大義今釋. Shanghai: Fudan Univ. Press, 2003.

Ohso (Bhagwan Shree Rajneesh). *The Heart Sutra: Talks on Sutras of Gautama the Buddha.* Berkeley, CA: Rebel Publishing House, 2008.

Red Pine. (tr. and comm.) *The Heart Sutra.* Washington, DC: Shoemaker & Hoard, 2004.

Sit, Kwan-yuk Claire. *Lao Tzu and Anthroposophy: A Translation of the Tao Te Ching with Commentary and a Lao Tzu Document "The Great One Excretes Water"* (2nd ed.). Great Barrington, MA: Lindisfarne Books, 2012.

———. *The Lord's Prayer: An Eastern Perspective.* Great Barrington, MA: SteinerBooks, 2008.

Smith, Edward Reaugh. *The Burning Bush: Rudolf Steiner, Anthroposophy, and the Holy Scriptures: Terms & Phrases.* Hudson, NY: Anthroposophic Press, 1998.

Sonam, Geshe (Ruth Sonam, tr.). *The Heart Sutra: An Oral Teaching by Geshe Sonam Rinchen.* Ithaca, NY: Snow Lion, 2003.

Soothill, William Edward, and Lewis Hodous (eds.). *A Dictionary of Chinese Buddhist Terms with Sanskrit and English Equivalents and a Sanskrit–Pali Index.* New York: RoutledgeCurzon, 1937 (paperback 2004).

Steiner, Rudolf. *According to Luke: The Gospel of Compassion and Love Revealed.* Great Barrington, MA: SteinerBooks, 2001.

———. *According to Matthew: The Gospel of Christ's Humanity.* Great Barrington, MA: SteinerBooks, 2002.

———. *Autobiography: Chapters in the Course of My Life, 1861–1907.* Great Barrington, MA: SteinerBooks, 2000.

———. *Background to the Gospel of St. Mark.* Hudson, NY: Anthroposophic Press, 1986.

———. *The Being of Man and His Future Evolution.* London: Rudolf Steiner Press, 1981.

———. *Christianity as Mystical Fact: And the Mysteries of Antiquity.* Great Barrington, MA: SteinerBooks, 2006.

———. *Das Geheimnis des Todes. Wesen und Bedeutung Mitteleuropas und die europäischen Volksgeister.* Basel: Rudolf Steiner Verlag, 2005.

———. *Esoteric Christianity and the Mission of Christian Rosenkreutz.* London: Rudolf Steiner Press, 2001.

———. *Esoteric Lessons 1910–1912: From the Esoteric School,* vol. 2. Great Barrington, MA: SteinerBooks, 2012.

———. *The Festivals and Their Meaning.* London: Rudolf Steiner Press, 1996.

———. *The Fifth Gospel: From the Akashic Record.* London: Rudolf Steiner Press, 1995.

Selected Bibliography

———. *The Foundations of Human Experience.* Hudson, NY: Anthroposophic Press, 1996.

———. *Genesis: Secrets of Creation.* London: Rudolf Steiner Press, 2002.

———. *The Gospel of St. John and its Relation to the other Gospels.* Hudson, NY: Anthroposophic Press, 1982.

———. *How to Know Higher Worlds: A Modern Path of Initiation.* Hudson, NY: Anthroposophic Press, 1994.

———. *The Influences of Lucifer and Ahriman: Human Responsibility for the Earth.* Hudson, NY: Anthroposophic Press, 1976 (rev. trans., 1993).

———. *The Influence of Spiritual Beings upon Man.* Hudson, NY: Anthroposophic Press, 1961.

———. *Man in the Light of Occultism, Theosophy and Philosophy.* London: Rudolf Steiner Press, 1964.

———. *Manifestations of Karma.* London: Rudolf Steiner Press, 1996.

———. *The Mission of the Folk-Souls: In Relation to Teutonic Mythology.* London: Rudolf Steiner Press, 2005.

———. *Mystery of the Sun and the Threefold Man* (unpublished typewritten manuscript).

———. *Mystery of the Universe: The Human Being, Model of Creation.* London: Rudolf Steiner Press, 2001.

———. *The Origin and Goal of the Human Being* (private printing).

———. *An Outline of Esoteric Science.* Hudson, NY: Anthroposophic Press, 1997.

———. *A Psychology of Body, Soul, and Spirit: Anthroposophy, Psychosophy, Pneumatosophy.* Hudson, NY: Anthroposophic Press, 1999.

———. *The Reappearance of Christ in the Etheric.* Great Barrington, MA: SteinerBooks, 2003.

———. *The Spiritual Hierarchies and the Physical World: Zodiac, Planets, and Cosmos.* Great Barrington, MA: SteinerBooks, 2008.

———. *Spiritual Science as a Foundation for Social Forms.* Hudson, NY: Anthroposophic Press, 1986.

———. *The Story of My Life.* Hudson, NY: Anthroposophic Press, 1928 (see Steiner, *Autobiography*).

———. *Supersensible Knowledge.* Hudson, NY: Anthroposophic Press, 1987.

———. *Theosophy: An Introduction to the Spiritual Processes in Human Life and in the Cosmos.* Hudson, NY: Anthroposophic Press, 1994.

———. *A Way of Self-knowledge: And the Threshold of the Spiritual World.* Great Barrington, MA: SteinerBooks, 1999.

———. *Wisdom of Man, of the Soul, and of the Spirit.* Hudson, NY: Anthroposophic Press, 1971 (see Steiner, *A Psychology of Body, Soul, and Spirit*).

———. *The World of the Senses: And the World of the Spirit.* London: Rudolf Steiner Press, 2014.

Studholme, Alexander. *The Origins of Om Manipadme Hum: A Study of the Karandavyuha Sutra.* Albany, NY: SUNY Press, 2002.

Sun, Xiaozhi 孫孝智. *Xin Jing Jie Du* 心經解讀. www.willyimage.com/calligraphy/TheHeartSutra.htm.

Teresa of Avila. *The Life of Teresa of Jesus.* Middlesex, UK: Echo Library, 2011.

Thich, Nhat Hanh. *The Heart of Perfect Understanding:* www.plumvillage.org/practice/mp3/98-the-heart-of-perfect-understanding.html.

Trungpa, Chögyam. *Born in Tibet.* New York: Harcourt, Brace & World, 1968.

Werner, E. T. C. *Myths and Legends of China.* New York: George G. Harrap, 1922.

Yoo, Dosung. *Thunderous Silence: A Formula for Ending Suffering.* Boston: Wisdom, 2013.

Zajonc, Arthur. *Catching the Light: The Entwined History of Light and Mind.* New York: Oxford University Press, 1993.

Zong Shao 宗紹 (ed.). *Chán-zōng Wú Mén Guān* 禪宗無門關: www.baus-ebs.org/sutra/fan-read/003/03-016.htm.

INDEX

Abraham 64
Absolute, the 14, 30, 31, 37, 38
aggregates, five 13, 18, 21, 24, 27, 28, 40
Ahura Mazda 56
akashic record 61, 75, 82
alaya-vijnana (ā lài yé shi) 40
Ananda (Ānán) 8
Anthroposophy (Spiritual Science) 7, 8, 35, 41, 54, 55, 56, 60, 61, 65, 75, 78
anuttara-samyak-sambodhi (unexcelled-complete-universal-enlightenment) 54
arhat (luó-hàn) 43, 55
as above, so below 30
Asia 8
astral body 56, 61, 73, 75, 76, 77, 78, 79, 81, 82
atheist 32
atma (spirit body) 80
A-U-M (om) 68
Avalokitesvara/Avalokita 13, 14, 15, 16, 17, 18, 19, 21, 24, 25, 28, 29, 38, 39, 44, 50, 53, 54, 67, 68, 71, 73, 74

Bā-Zhèng-Dào (Eightfold Path) 33, 43, 51
benefit 8, 44, 52, 61, 73
benefit self to benefit others 13
beyond, the 20, 21, 24, 28, 53, 72, 73
biàn-lì (convenience, expedient means) 39, 52, 73
blessing(s) 22, 52, 68, 74
bodhi (perfect wisdom) 13, 20, 45, 51, 67, 71, 72
bodhi tree 45, 49, 60
Bodhidharma (First Patriarch of Zen) 44
bō rě (prajna) 19, 20
bō-rě bō-luó-mì duō (prajnaparamita) 19
Buddha, Amitabha (Ē-mí-tuó Fó), 68, 70
Buddhism, Hinayana 6, 44
Buddhism, Mahayana 6, 10, 44, 51, 67
Buddhism, Pure Land 68
Buddhism, Tibetan 23, 52, 68, 69

Buddhism, Zen 44, 45, 46, 47, 49, 70
Buddhist(s) 5, 6, 8, 9, 10, 13, 14, 22, 23, 24, 25, 26, 38, 39, 41, 43, 44, 52, 55, 56, 57, 60, 67, 68, 73
Budhi 55
bù-shī (charity, dana) 20

calligrapher 5, 47, 48
calligraphy 5, 6, 47
cān gōng'-àn (meditate on a koan) 47
cān huà-tóu (meditate on a pivoting word or phrase of a koan) 47
causes of suffering (jí) 42
chán-dìng (mediation, dhyana) 20
cháng-lè-wǒ-jìng ("eternity, joy, the Self, and purity") 53
charity (bù-shī, dana) 20, 52
chí-jiè (moral discipline, sila) 20
Chikai 26
China 10, 22, 44, 47, 48, 70
Chinese 5, 9, 10, 11, 15, 19, 22, 27, 34, 57
Chödrön, Pema 52
Chrestos 55
Christ 8, 56, 57, 60, 63, 64, 65, 77, 78, 80, 81
Christ, Cosmic 8
Christianity 60, 62, 63, 65
Christianity, esoteric 7, 60, 62, 63, 65
Chún-yáng-zi (Pure-yang-fellow), *see* Lǚ Dòngbīn 23
clairvoyance/clairvoyant 31, 34, 55, 63, 77
consciousness, 7th (klista-mano) 40
consciousness, 8th (alaya-vijnana) 40
consciousness, deep-trance 79, 80
consciousness, dream-filled sleep 79, 80
consciousness, dreamless-sleep 79, 80
consciousness(es) 14, 18, 19, 24, 30, 34, 37, 40, 41, 56, 60, 72, 74, 78, 79
Consciousness, Sea of 19
Consciousness, Universal 14, 18, 19, 24, 55, 56, 57, 72
consciousness, waking 79, 80
Cosmic Buddha 8

cosmic knowledge 7, 8
cosmos 7, 55, 61, 75, 77

Dà Bānnièpán Jīng (The Mahaparinirvana Sutra) 53
dà cí-bēi (great mercy) 19, 73
Dalai Lama, The (Tenzin Gatso) 23, 72
dana (charity, bù shī) 20
dào (means of liberation from suffering) 43
dà-zì-zài (greatly free and comfortable) 19, 73
delusion(s) 20, 51, 53, 54, 70, 72, 73
dependent origination (yuán-qǐ) 6, 32, 35, 42
Dharma Realm 16
dharma(s) 26, 37, 38, 39, 45, 49, 50, 52, 60, 72, 73
dhyana (meditation, chán dìng) 20
Diamond Sutra, The (Jīn-gāng Jīng) 33, 44, 46, 50, 58, 70, 71, 74
Dong Chu Old Monk 9
Dūnhuáng 45

ear 37, 40
ear-entrance 16, 18
ear, spiritual 18
Earth 80
egoism/egoistic 40, 57, 81
eighteen-element (shí-bā-jiè) 41
Eightfold Path (Bā-Zhèng-Dào) 33, 43, 51
Eight Immortals, The 22
Elijah 64
emptiness, *see also* form 16, 25, 28, 29, 30, 31, 32, 34, 35, 37, 38, 39, 45, 46, 49, 50, 72, 73
emptiness, semblance of 37, 38, 72, 73
empty 13, 16, 18, 21, 24, 27, 28, 31, 32, 38, 39, 40, 45, 46, 71, 73
endurance (rěn-rǔ, kshanti) 20
enlightened/enlightenment 13, 14, 16, 20, 32, 33, 34, 44, 45, 46, 47, 48, 49, 50, 51, 53, 54, 60, 68, 70, 71, 72, 73
esotericism 18, 24
essence (yǒu) 20, 29, 31, 35
Essene 63

"eternity, joy, the Self, and purity" (cháng-lè-wǒ-jìng) 53, 72, 74
etheric body 56, 57, 61, 73, 75, 76, 77, 78, 79, 81, 82
etheric (life) principle 61, 65, 76, 84
evolution 56, 72, 75, 78, 79, 80, 81, 82, 83
evolution, Earth phase 78, 79, 80, 82, 83, 84
evolution, Jupiter phase 78, 79, 80
evolution, old Moon phase 78, 79, 80, 83, 84
evolution, old Saturn phase 78, 79, 80, 82
evolution, old Sun phase 78, 79, 80
evolution, Venus phase 78, 79, 80
evolution, Vulcan phase 78, 80
expedient means, convenience (biàn-lì) 20, 39, 50, 52, 73
eye(s) 21, 22, 26, 33, 37, 40, 41
eye, sound 23, 24
eye, spiritual 18, 21, 22, 23, 24

Fǎhuá Jīng (The Lotus Sutra) 15
Fifth Patriarch of Zen (Hóngrěn) 44, 70
finger, cutting off 49, 73
finger, koan of raising a 49
First Patriarch of Zen (Bodhidharma) 44
five-no-translation rule 10
flesh, three ounces of 58, 59
form, *see also* emptiness 15, 21, 25, 27, 28, 29, 30, 31, 32, 34, 35, 37, 40, 42, 68, 72, 73
Fó Shuī Dà-chéng Zhuāng-yán Bǎo Wáng Jīng (Karandavyuha Sutra) 67
Four Noble Truths, The (Sì-Shèng-Dì) 42, 51
fractal 30, 36
free and comfortable (zì-yóu-zì-zài) 19, 28, 73

gate (gone) 4, 67, 72
Gautama Buddha 14, 15, 16, 20, 32, 33, 34, 38, 39, 41, 42, 44, 53, 57, 58, 59, 60, 61, 62, 68
God 14, 23, 32, 42
Golden-Flower 22, 23
Golgotha, *see also* Mystery of Golgotha 8, 57, 63, 64, 78

Index

Gospel of John 23
Gospel of Luke 65
Gospel of Matthew 23
great mercy (dà cí-bēi) 19, 73
greatly free and comfortable (dà-zì-zài) 19, 73
Guān-shì-yīn (Guān-yīn), *see also* Avalokitesvara 14, 15
Guān-shì-yīn, Nā-mó ~ pú-sà 18, 67
Guān-yīn Rú-lái (Tathagata Observer of Sounds) 16
Guān-zì-zài, *see also* Avalokitesvara 14, 15, 19

Heart Sutra, The (*Xin-jing*) 18, 19, 20, 24, 25, 30, 38, 40, 47, 48, 49, 50, 51, 67, 71, 73, 74
hierarchies, spiritual 78, 79, 81, 82, 83, 84
Hinduism 68
"Homage to Bodhisattva Avalokitesvara" (Nā-mó Guān-shì-yīn pú-sà) 18, 67
"Homage to Buddha Amitabha" (Nā-mó Ē-mí-tuó-fó) 68
Hóngrěn (Fifth Patriarch of Zen) 44, 70
Huáng-méi, county of 70
Huìnéng (Sixth Patriarch of Zen) 44, 45, 46, 70, 71
human/humanity/humankind 17, 18, 23, 31, 32, 34, 41, 42, 46, 56, 57, 60, 61, 62, 65, 72, 73, 75, 76

"I"/"I"-being 56, 61, 63, 75, 76, 77, 78, 79, 80
ice patch 19, 55, 56
Imagination (psychic) consciousness 79, 80
immaterial nature (xìng-kōng) 32
immortal (shén-xiān) 22
incarnated 14, 54, 62
India/Indian 8, 9, 10, 32, 44, 47, 56, 59, 62
Indian rishis 56
initiate 7, 8, 77
inner light 22, 23, 24, 28, 31, 52
Inspiration (super-psychic) consciousness 79, 80
Intuition (spiritual) consciousness 80

Jeshu ben Pandira 63
Jesus, as a youth 60, 62, 65
Jesus, birth 61
Jesus, child 61
Jesus Christ 23, 52, 57, 63, 64
Jesus of Nazareth 57, 63
jí (causes of suffering) 42
Jīn-gāng Jīng (*The Diamond Sutra*) 33
jīng jìn (zeal and habit, virya) 20
Jordan River 57, 63
Jung, Carl 76
Jùzhī, Zen Master 49, 73

Karandavyuha Sutra, The, (*Fó Shuì Dà-chéng Zhuāng-yán Bǎo Wáng Jīng*) 67
kingdom, animal 35, 75, 76, 78, 80
kingdom, mineral 35, 75, 76, 78, 80
kingdom, plant 35, 75, 76, 78, 80
klista-mano (mò nà shi) 40
koan (gōng'-àn) 46, 48, 49
koan meditation (cān gōng'-àn) 47
kshanti (endurance, rěn-rǔ) 20
kǔ (suffering) 42
Kucha (Qiū-cí) 10
Kumarajiva (1st translator of *The Heart Sutra*) 10, 14, 27

Lankavatara Sutra, The (*Léng-jiā Jīng*) 44
Laozi 29, 33, 34
Léng-jiā Jīng (*The Lankavatara Sutra*) 44
Léng-yán Jīng (*The Surangama Sutra*) 16
liberation from suffering (miè) 42
lì, biàn- (convenience) 39, 73
life spirit (buddhi) 79
lì, fú- (benefit) 52, 73
light, clear 23, 28, 31
light experiment 21
light, inner 22, 23, 24, 28, 31, 52
light, unmanifest 24, 30, 37, 74
Li Shì-mín (Taizong of Tang Dynasty) 15
liù-chén (six-dust) 40
liù-gēn (six-root) 40
liù-jiè (six-element) 40
lì-yì (profit) 27, 38, 51, 73
Lord of Observation, *see also* Avalokitesvara 14

Lotus Sutra, The (*Fǎhuá Jīng*) 15
luó-*hàn* (arhat) 43
Lusthaus, Dan 10

Mahaparinirvana Sutra, The (*Dà Bānnièpán Jīng*) 53, 58, 59
Maitreya Buddha (Mílè Fó) 57, 62, 63, 64, 65
Maitreya (Mílè) 14, 57, 60, 64, 65
Majjhima Nikaya (*Zhōng-ā-hán Jīng*) 60
manas (spirit self) 79
Manjusri (Wénshū) 14
mantra, six-syllable 67, 68
maya 35, 36, 38, 49, 52, 53
means of liberation from suffering (dào) 43
meditation 16, 18, 19, 20, 21, 22, 23, 24, 26, 28, 44, 45, 47, 71
meditation on a koan (cān gōng'-àn) 47
meditation on a pivoting word or phrase of a koan (cān huà-tóu) 47
meditation using the process of hearing and reflecting 16, 24
miè (liberation from suffering) 42
Mílè Fó (Buddha Maitreya) 57
Mílè (Maitreya) 57
moral discipline (chí-jiè, sila) 20
Moses 64
Mystery of Golgotha 57, 63, 64

"Nā-mó Ē-mí-tuó-fó" (Homage to Amitabha Buddha) 68
"Nā-mó Guān-shì-yīn pú-sà" (Homage to Bodhisattva Avalokitesvara) 18, 67
niè-pán (nirvana) 14
Nirmanakaya (Yīng-huà-shēn) 61
nirvana (niè-pán) 14, 20, 51, 53, 54, 59, 72, 73
nothingness (wú) 29

Observer of the World's Sounds, *see also* Avalokitesvara 16
occultism 55
om (A-U-M) 67, 68
"om mani padme hum" 67
Ōuyáng Xún 47, 48

Pali 8

perfection of wisdom (prajnaparamita) 13, 18, 19, 20, 24, 25, 27, 36, 40, 44, 51, 53, 54, 67, 71, 72
perfect wisdom (bodhi), *see also* prajna 13, 14, 20, 51
Persians, ancient 56
persist–resist principle 46
physical body 56, 61, 63, 73, 75, 76, 77, 78, 79, 80, 81, 82
physical world 28, 31, 35, 38, 53, 54
pinyin system of romanization 11
Platform Sutra of the Sixth Patriarch, The 45, 70, 71
prajna (wisdom, bō-rě) 19, 20, 70
prajnaparamita (bō-rě bō-luó-mì duō), *see also* perfection of wisdom 19, 20, 71, 72
Prajnaparamita Heart Sutra, The, *see also The Heart Sutra* 5
Prajnaparamita Mantra, The 71
Prajnaparamita Sutras, The 20, 38
Pratyeka-Buddhas (Pì-zhī Fó) 55
profit (lì-yì) 27, 28, 36, 38, 48, 51, 52, 73
Pure-yang-fellow (Chún-yáng-zi), *see* Lǚ Dòngbīn 23
pú-tí-sà-duǒ (pú-sà, bodhisattva) 13, 15
Pǔxián (Samantabhadra) 14
Pythagoreans 68

Qiū-cí (Kucha) 10

Ramakrishna, Sri 32
Rándēng Fó (Dīpankara Buddha) 57, 58
real being (zhēnrén) 22
realm 16, 20, 41
rěn-rǔ (endurance, kshanti) 20
right-mindedness, Buddha of 65
Rú-lái (one who has thus come), *see also* Tathagata 16, 56
Rú-qù (one who has thus gone), *see also* Tathagata 56

Samantabhadra (Pǔxián) 14
samsara (shēng-sǐ, birth and death) 14, 16, 20, 42, 43, 51, 59
Sanskrit 8, 9, 10, 11, 13, 14, 19, 37
sarika 25, 26

Index

Sariputra (Shè-lì-zi) 25, 26, 27, 28, 37, 38, 39, 40, 43, 44, 50, 51, 73
sarira(s) 25, 26
sattva 13
Self 53, 72, 74
selfless 18
self-similar 30
sense consciousness 41
sense(s) 16, 27, 34, 40, 41, 42
senses, six 41
senses, twelve 41
sentient being(s) 13, 19, 20, 44, 55, 59, 60, 68, 73
Shakyamuni, *see also* Buddha Gautama 7, 57, 58, 59
Shè-lì-zi (Sariputra) 6, 25, 27, 36, 39, 50, 51, 73
shēng-sǐ (birth and death, samsara) 14
shén-xiān (immortal) 22
Shénxiù 45, 46, 71
shí-bā-jiè (eighteen-element) 41
shí'-èr-yīn-yuán (twelve causes) 42
shore 20
Sierpinski triangle 30, 32, 38
sila (moral discipline, chí-jiè) 20
Silk Road 10
Sì-Shèng-Dì (Four Noble Truths) 42, 51
six-dust (liù-chén) 40
six-element (liù-jiè) 40
six-root (liù-gēn) 40
six senses 41
six-syllable mantra 67, 68
Sixth Patriarch of Zen (Huìnéng) 44, 45, 46, 70, 71
Song Dynasty 9, 47
Sons of Life 83
soul, consciousness 7, 81, 82
soul, intellectual (or mind) 7, 81, 82
soul, sentient 7, 81, 82
spirit human (atma) 80
spirit self (manas) 79
Spirits of Fire 83
Spirits of Form 35, 83, 84
Spirits of Harmony 83
Spirits of Love 83
Spirits of Motion 83, 84
Spirits of Personality 83, 84
Spirits of Will 83

Spirits of Wisdom 83, 84
spiritual ear 18
spiritual eye 18, 21, 23, 24
Spiritual Science (Anthroposophy) 75
Steiner, Rudolf 7, 8, 21, 24, 26, 32, 33, 34, 35, 41, 42, 43, 54, 56, 57, 60, 61, 63, 64, 65, 72, 75, 77, 82
suffering (kǔ) 5, 13, 15, 19, 28, 37, 42, 52, 53, 59, 67, 68, 72, 74
Sun 82
Sun Hero 55
Sun Soul 56, 57, 72
suprasensory 21, 24, 28, 35

tableau, life 77
Taizong (of the Tang Dynasty) 15
Tang Dynasty 15
tantric 68
Tao 14, 29, 34
Taoism/Taoist(s) 21, 22, 30, 36, 73
Tao Te Ching, The 29, 30, 34, 35, 36, 38, 82
tapasya (religious austerity) 32
Tathagata Observer of Sounds (Guān-yīn Rú-lái) 16
Tathagata (Rú-lái) 16, 33, 38, 56, 58, 59, 60
Teacher of the Good 64
Teresa of Avila, St. 24
thousand-hand form (Avalokitesvara) 17
Three Times, the 51, 54, 57
thus come (Rú-lái) 56
thus gone (Rú-qù) 56
"Thus have I heard" 8
tonglen (taking and giving) 52
Trungpa, Chögyam 14
twelve causes (shí'-èr-yīn-yuán) 42, 43
twelve senses 41

unexcelled-complete-universal-enlightenment (anuttara-samyak-sambodhi), 51, 54, 72, 73
Universal Consciousness 14, 18, 19, 24, 55, 56, 72
unlearning 40
unmanifest light 24, 30, 37, 74
unspoken word, the 24, 30, 37, 74

virya (zeal and habit, jīng jìn) 20

Vishva Karman 56

Wade-Giles (system of Romanization) 11
Wénshū (Manjusri) 14
Western World of Eternal Bliss 68
wisdom, perfection of (prajnaparamita)
    13, 14, 18, 19, 20, 24, 25, 27, 36,
    40, 44, 51, 53, 54, 67, 71, 72
word, the unspoken 24, 30, 37, 74
wú (nothingness) 29

xìng-kōng (immaterial nature) 32
Xuánzàng 10, 14, 27, 47, 48

yang 21, 31
yin 21, 31
Yīng-huà-shēn (Nirmanakaya) 61
yŏu (essence) 29, 42
yuán-qǐ (conditional causation) 6, 32

Zajonc, Arthur 21
zeal and habit (jīng jìn, virya) 20, 43
Zen 44, 45, 47, 49, 70
Zen, Fifth Patriarch of, (Hóngrěn) 44, 70

Zen, First Patriarch of, (Bodhidharma) 44
Zen, Sixth Patriarch of, (Huìnéng) 44, 45, 46, 70, 71
zhēn-rén (real being) 22
Zhōng-ā-hán Jīng (*Majjhima Nikaya*) 60
zì-lì-lì-tā (benefit self to benefit others) 13, 52
zì-yóu-zì-zài (free and comfortable) 19, 28, 73

www.ingramcontent.com/pod-product-compliance
Lightning Source LLC
Chambersburg PA
CBHW020947090426
42736CB00010B/1305